# Happy Parenting!

# Happy Parenting!

**From Infancy to Young Adulthood**

## James & Mary Kenny

Cover, book design and illustrations by Julie V. Lonneman.

SBN 0-86716-005-5

# Contents

# Foreword

This book is a collection of columns on the blessings and
problems of parenting and child care. The columns began in
1976 at the invitation of the National Catholic News Service.
They were syndicated under the title "Family Talk."

"Family Talk" grew like Topsy, every which way.
Readers wrote in questions in greater and greater numbers,
and we tried to provide answers. There was no particular
order. They came at random. It was quite stimulating to
carry on a spontaneous dialogue with our readers. We owe
them much.

After a while we discovered that we had written quite a
bit on parenthood. We divided these columns into five
chapters encompassing the ages and stages from infancy to
adulthood. Within each age are many special topics and
problems which can quickly be located through the index at
the end of the book. We devoted the two final chapters to
topics which might arise at any age in childhood: adoption
and discipline. There is some unity, yet we hope the book
retains its original rather haphazard responsiveness.

Where did we learn all about family life? More than
anywhere else, from experience. Our academic learning has
always been tempered by reality, and in life experience we
have had the very best teachers in the world. We are grateful
to our 12 children who taught us most of what we know and
to whom this book is dedicated.

Finally, we must confess that we have had fun writing
these columns. Children are our favorite topic. Imagine
writing on your favorite topic and getting paid for it!

We hope these questions and answers will help you in
your adventure as parents. We believe these collected
columns make an original contribution to the plethora of
manuals on childrearing because we write as *Christian*
parents committed to Christian values in family life.

Happy reading—and happy parenting!

# Birth to Two
# Infants

Infancy is a precious experience, a brief moment in life when needs and wants are synonymous. Holding and physical touch are vital. Spoiling is probably impossible. In one sense the parenting of infants is easy: It amounts to unconditional love.

# Spoiling

**What do you think about spoiling babies? When my baby cries, I pick her up. I hold her a great deal, and some people say I'm spoiling her. Am I?**

You're caught in the middle of an age-old dilemma—to let baby cry or to pick her up? We are 100 percent on your side. Pick up your baby. If we look at the nature of infants, I think you'll understand why.

The first clue that crying is not good for babies is that crying bothers us. The sound of infant crying upsets any human being, male or female, big or little. Since this reaction is universal, I think we can justly interpret it as a natural signal: "This baby needs something. Do something." If you need further convincing that crying bothers us, observe older children. An adult might put off a crying baby, even claim crying is "good" for the baby. A child never will. A child quickly and insistently announces to the mother, "The baby's crying!"

Perhaps one reason we adults feel we should put off a crying baby is that we see crying as "bad" behavior. That is what your critics mean when they say, "Let your baby cry or you'll spoil her." Crying is "bad" only from the adult viewpoint. From the baby's viewpoint crying is communication. Books, workshops, therapy sessions abound to teach people how to communicate. It seems inconsistent to ignore this very little person's efforts to communicate.

Does holding spoil babies? Again we like to look to nature for the answer. Almost everyone has observed young puppies or kittens. They snuggle close to their litter mates and stay with the mother almost constantly. Separation from mother and siblings is the ultimate in distress. In the animal kingdom it seems almost universal that newborns need mother, not occasionally, not when she has time for them, not on a four-hour schedule, but almost constantly. Why do we think that new human babies should be happy alone in a large crib in a private room? When your baby asks to be held and snuggled, she is demonstrating the new baby's need for warmth, cuddling, human contact. This need exists more or less on a 24-hour-a-day basis.

Your baby needs to be held, touched. The skin is an organ. Research suggests that skin stimulation is not simply a nice extra between mother and baby, but a need as vital as food and warmth. So hold, touch, stroke, enjoy.

Of course this does not mean a mother ought to do nothing but hold her baby 24 hours a day. Comforting a new baby is not as impossible as it sounds. The younger the baby, the greater the need to be held. This fits in beautifully with the mother's own need. In the early days and weeks after birth, she spends the most time with her baby. This is the time when she can and should have an easy work schedule to relax and enjoy her baby. If she is tired, she can crawl into bed with baby to rest or nap. A baby snuggled close to mom will usually oblige by dropping off to sleep.

As the baby grows, he still needs mother but less constantly. Daddy and other soothing, loving relatives and friends make wonderful baby holders. Slings and carriers enable mother to fasten baby on her. Carriers are indispensable for walking, shopping, or for use around the house. Baby nestles close to mother in utmost contentment, and mother has a free hand to do what needs to be done.

As the weeks pass, baby becomes increasingly aware of his surroundings. He then enjoys short periods in an infant seat, preferably, in the center of the household where he can watch the action. When he has had enough and wants cuddling or sleep, he will let you know.

When a child reaches 18 months or two years, we begin to have certain expectations and make certain demands on her. Then it is quite possible to spoil. But now we are talking about babies, and babies are to love. The time when baby needs mother all the time is actually very short. Enjoy your baby. You can't spoil a baby by giving him what he needs. You might, however, spoil a baby by *not* giving him what he needs.

# Breastfeeding

**My daughter is expecting her first baby and wants to breastfeed. I was not able to breastfeed my babies. Is there any way I can help her be more successful than I was?**

Tell your daughter that you applaud her decision. Breastfeeding offers several advantages both for mother and baby. Nutritionally, breast milk is the ideal food for the human infant. Cow's milk formula frequently cannot be tolerated, but there is no such thing as breast-milk intolerance. Recognizing these nutritional advantages, both the American and Canadian pediatric associations recently advised their members actively to encourage mothers to breastfeed. (One pediatrician who has encouraged breastfeeding for many years called this move "reinventing the wheel.")

In addition, a successful breastfeeding experience is psychologically good for mother and baby. Many mothers report that breastfeeding brings them close to their babies and gives them great personal satisfaction.

Breastfeeding is also convenient. There are no bottles to wash or haul around. And it is inexpensive. The cost of formula is considerable during the first year of life.

Can any mother breastfeed? One wise physician says there are only three types of mothers who cannot: mothers who are addicted to hard drugs, mothers who have active tuberculosis, and mothers who say, "I don't want to."

Why do mothers who want to breastfeed frequently give up? Recent research on breastfeeding offers three reasons:

1) *Misinformation*. Some mothers fear—wrongly—that

4

they cannot produce enough milk, that their milk is too watery, or that their baby is eating too often. Encourage your daughter to read about breastfeeding and to talk to mothers who have breastfed so that she has correct information.

2) *Mismanagement.* Breastfeeding is a supply and demand system. Breast milk digests quickly, and breastfed infants normally eat every couple of hours. To attempt to nourish breastfed infants on a four-hour schedule or to expect them to sleep through the night is tampering with nature's schedule. Breastfed babies do best staying close to mom and eating on demand.

3) *Lack of support.* First-time moms are apt to blame themselves for any problems with their baby. For some unknown reason, breastfeeding moms, their friends and even their doctors frequently blame breastfeeding for their problems. With such lack of confidence and support, moms often stop breastfeeding. Be a positive supporter of your daughter. She needs your confidence in her.

La Leche League is an organization whose sole purpose is to promote "good mothering through breastfeeding." It gives information. support and encouragement to mothers who want to breastfeed. Its manual, *The Womanly Art of Breastfeeding,* is available from La Leche League International, Inc., 9616 Minneapolis Avenue, Franklin Park, Illinois 60131. Information on breastfeeding support groups throughout the world is available from the same address. Encourage your daughter to find support for breastfeeding from other mothers.

If she is adequately informed and supported, your daughter can breastfeed successfully and enjoy one of the happiest experiences of mothering.

# Sleeping With Parents

When our babies were little, I took them into bed with my

husband and me if they were restless during the night. Also during thunderstorms or bad dreams we have always permitted our children to crawl into bed with us. I have read some advice that this is a very bad practice for children. What do you think?

If sleeping with parents is a very bad practice for children, I doubt the human race would ever have survived. Much of the advice on childrearing in the 20th century has warned against this "bad practice." The one group that never read the advice and never found the practice "bad" was the children. Babies and young children persist in thinking, "When I need mama, I need mama." The time of day has nothing to do with it. Although frequently frowned on in our culture, some parents continue to take children into the parental bed.

Why is this practice considered bad? Often it is referred to as a bad *habit*. (If you let an infant sleep with you, you will never get him out of the parental bed. Therefore, never let him in.) Parents who do permit their children in their bed know from experience that this is simply not so. As the child grows, she proceeds from sleeping with mommy and daddy to joining an older brother or sister, to wanting a bed of her own. This entire process may take years, but it does surely come about.

Another objection is that parents have no privacy. They have no opportunity for private conversation or for loving. Come now! Children are not awake in the parental bed at all times. When children are in the parents' bed, mom and dad simply develop their own ingenuity in finding times and places for privacy and sex.

Another argument is that parents need their sleep. Any mother will tell you that there is no drain on sleep comparable to getting up hourly trying to comfort a restless child. Take that child into your bed, and everyone can get some sleep.

The basic, often unspoken taboo against bringing children into the parental bed has to do with touching and intimacy. Until recent years our culture has had great reservations about touching. All touching was interpreted as sexual. As Desmond Morris wrote in his book *Intimate Behavior:* "This stress on the sexual element in all forms of intimate behavior has resulted in a massive inhibition of our non-sexual body intimacies. When these intimacies apply to parents and offspring, then beware, Oedipus! To siblings, beware, incest! To close same-sex friends, beware, homosexuality! To close opposite-sex friends, beware, adultery! And to many casual friends, beware, promiscuity!" With such a list of taboos, is it any wonder that we ban children from the parental bed?

Freud wrote that children witnessing the "primal scene" would suffer from neuroses or worse. Hence, in modern America, we have Dr. Spock declaring emphatically that children should be out of the parents' room (much less their bed) and into a room of their own by no later than six months of age.

Despite all the adverse warnings, parents—often secretively—take their children into their bed. Babies love it. Mothers, who hour after hour have tried to coax a restless child into "his own bed," suddenly feel the peace, security and satisfaction of having family members physically close. They then realize: This is right.

Night-crying is not the selfish demand of a spoiled child, but expresses a child's need for comfort, security and human touch. It is quite different from the spoiled child's demand for candy. Meeting this need is not spoiling. This is parenting: calmly reassuring the child that mama and daddy are here, you are safe, and all's well with the world.

A beautiful book discussing at length the entire issue is *The Family Bed* by Tine Thevenin. It is available from Tine Thevenin, P.O. Box 16004, Minneapolis, Minnesota 55416.

# Night-Waking

Our 16-month-old little boy has rarely slept all night since he was six months old. We put him on a full-size mattress on the floor beside our bed and for two nights he slept all night. When we put the mattress into a frame, he woke up several times and would only sleep with us. He has two sisters, eight and four. I've tried letting the oldest one sleep with him, putting the mattress on the floor and giving him medicine for worms. Nothing works. I am pregnant again and wonder how we can help him sleep alone. Our doctor says he is spoiled and should be allowed to cry. I just can't do that. He seems only semi-awake and cries like he is scared. We also have a lot of pressure put on us because he sleeps with us.

You are obviously parents who are centered upon your baby's needs. Your letter does not ask, "How can I get a good night's sleep?" (although I'm sure you would enjoy one), but rather, "How can I help my baby?" There is a world of difference between the two approaches. Your approach leads to meeting the child's needs.

Sleep problems are more common than most parents admit. The first question most new parents hear is, "Is he/she a good baby?" The next question explains what is meant by *good:* "Does he/she sleep through the night?"

Most infants in human history have slept with their siblings. Night-waking by children and adults was normal and natural. No one was supposed to sleep through the night. Always another person was close by for comfort.

In our culture, however, people are expected to sleep alone and sleep well. Babies a few weeks old are bedded alone and expected to sleep through the night. If an older child such as your 16-month-old does not sleep through the night, he is "spoiled." Yet a wife may find that, when her husband is away overnight, she does not sleep well. Interestingly, a wakeful child is spoiled. A wakeful adult has insomnia.

You need the support of other parents who believe that meeting a child's needs is not spoiling but parenting. You need the reassurance that other parents *do* get up night after night and that, eventually, the child will become a better sleeper—if he is not made anxious by being pushed. I suggest you contact the La Leche League (9616 Minneapolis Ave., Franklin Park, Illinois 60131) for a list of their literature and for the location of a support group in your area.

# Discipline for Babies

**I have a 10-month-old boy and want him to be well-behaved but not "abused." Please send me a copy of your article "Of Course We Punish Children," so I might use the appropriate discipline for my child.**

Wanting a child to be well-behaved but not abused is a fine goal of discipline. The article you requested, however, is directed toward older children. In regard to children as young as your son, our theme is, "Of course we don't punish babies."

Children under one year are babies. There are two basic reasons we don't punish babies. The task of the first year of life is to establish a secure, trusting relationship between parents and baby, especially between mother and baby. Erik Erikson, a psychoanalyist particularly concerned with human development, says that a basic attitude of trust or mistrust develops in the first year of life. The baby senses either, "The world is an O.K. place. You can count on it," or, "The world doesn't meet your needs. You can't trust it." This "world" Erikson refers to is the home environment which especially the mother creates.

For babies, wants and needs are synonymous. This means if baby is hungry, it is good to feed him. If he is tired, it is good to let him rest. If he wants someone to hold him, it

9

is good to hold him. This is not spoiling. It is meeting baby's needs.

The second reason we do not punish babies is that humans cannot learn something before they are mentally ready to learn it. Babies simply cannot grasp messages such as, "Don't put that in your mouth," "Don't go in that room." Even if the child develops some dim grasp of the message, teaching before the child is ready to learn requires 10 times the effort needed later. The cost may be higher than the premature learning is worth.

Punishing babies is inappropriate and ineffective. Infancy is the only time in raising children when the child's wants and needs are synonymous. Enjoy it. Concentrate on meeting your baby's needs. You cannot spoil a child under one year.

Obviously, however, a crawling infant cannot have free rein everywhere. Mother's appropriate action is to child-proof the environment. Get all the hazardous and breakable items out of baby's reach. Put away the bric-a-brac—and have that much less to dust. If stairs are a hazard, use a gate. If you don't want baby in the kitchen cabinets, tie them shut. If baby spots something he cannot have, distract him. If he spies the carving knife, give him the shiny measuring spoons instead. This kind of prevention is the appropriate form of discipline for babies.

Playpens are an obvious way to keep baby and the house safe; creeping, crawling and exploring, however, are ways that baby grows. Too much playpen can hamper this growth. Many families with several children find that they use the playpen less with each child as the house becomes more child-proofed and the parents become more relaxed. At any rate, be sure that baby gets some chance to roam free.

# Two to Six
# Preschoolers

From ornery at two until off-to-school at six is a long way to toddle. The task is considerable: The child must break away from complete dependence on parents and prepare for the first foray into the outside world. Temper tantrums, toilet training, problems at mealtime, selfishness and unbridled energy are almost universal issues. Parents want to know how to throw birthday parties and find baby-sitters, how to pick nursery schools, and when is a child ready for kindergarten? From a helpless infant, the child grows to a mobile little creature with a will of her own and the energy to move in many directions.

# Making Toddlers Behave

I find myself constantly spanking my 18-month-old because she will not obey simple commands like, "Come here!," "Stay out!" (out of drawers, cupboards, etc.), and "Don't scream!" She just stands there saying no or completely ignoring me.

I realize I am not a patient person. (So far I've only spanked her.) But I hate myself terribly after spanking her. Why can't I go just one day without spanking or hollering at her? Am I sick? After all, she is only a baby and she should be happy and full of smiles and laughter.

I love her so very much and I want her to grow up happy, wanting to be with her parents, and having fond childhood memories. These are things I don't have. My husband I get along very well and he is great with her. I hope you can help me before it is too late.

Thank you for your vivid account. You clearly point out that life with young children is not all sweetness and roses. We certainly do not think it is too late. We see some real strengths in you, and you can build on these to become a good parent.

Despite an unhappy childhood, you are coping as an adult. You recognize you are not patient. Each of us has developed different personality traits. It is not the tendency to impatience which is wrong, but acting on that impatience in ways that hurt others. You are distressed because you spank your baby all the time. Let us take the situations you describe and choose other means of discipline.

First, she won't "come here." An 18-month-old child is at the very earliest stage of discipline. Although toddlers know a few words, they are basically physical creatures. Thus, to be effective you make all your discipline *physical* but without spanking. In this case, when you say "come here," simply go get her. At age three or four she will come in response to your verbal command, but not yet.

Second, she won't "stay out of drawers, cabinets, etc." An 18-month-old sees no reason to stay out of the most fascinating places in the home. There is no way you can convince her otherwise. One response might be to invoke fear of dire punishment, a course you do not wish to take. A better way is to child-proof. Tie cabinets together. Lock drawers. Put valuable things up high. If she loves pots and pans, let her open that one kitchen cabinet and play with them. They are the cheapest, most sturdy toys around. Getting into everything is perfectly normal for a toddler, and it passes as she grows older.

Third, she won't "stop screaming." Everyone from the littlest baby to the oldest senior citizen loves attention. Your daughter has discovered how to get it. If you really want her to stop, the most effective course is to ignore it. Screaming will not disappear immediately, but if it fails to draw attention, it is much less fun. No attention, no screaming.

Finally, a word about spanking. You mention that you are short on patience, that you hate yourself for spanking, and that you have only spanked so far. For you and for any parent who fears losing control when spanking a child, we strongly recommend that you never spank. The danger of losing control and physically abusing your child is too great. To recognize your tendency is simply honest and wise. Instead try the techniques mentioned above: Carry out commands physically, child-proof, and ignore undesirable behavior.

# Two-Year-Olds and Mealtimes

This may seem like a small matter, but it bothers me very much. We have one child, an active two-year-old boy who is destroying our mealtime. Mark asks for food all through the day, but at dinner he eats very little. He plays with his food and he wants to get up and run around during dinner. An hour later he says he is hungry. This behavior bothers my husband. He blames me for Mark's behavior and says I don't discipline him. My husband gets so mad he cannot enjoy his dinner.

Frequent eating in small quantities all through the day is typical of preschool children. Frequent small meals may actually be better for us than three large meals per day. At any rate there is nothing wrong with snacking provided the snacks consist of nutritious food.

Since you control the kitchen, the control of Mark's eating behavior is in your hands. You have two choices with regard to snacking. If feeding Mark all day long bothers you very much, you can insist that he eat three times per day at mealtimes.

Your other choice, and the one we prefer, is to go along with Mark's snacking behavior. Give him good, nutritious snacks and keep them simple so you need not do extra preparation. Then let him eat as his hunger dictates. Choose fresh fruit; raw vegetables, cut and ready to eat; whole-grain breads and cereals; peanuts or popcorn; a glass of milk or real (not sugared) fruit juice.

What about the mealtime behavior? Playing with food and jumping up from the table are annoying to adults. Such behavior, however, lasts for only a short time in the child's life. You have several choices which would make your husband's dinnertime more pleasant.

First, you might feed Mark early. At your dinnertime, just give him a small plate and some finger-foods to nibble. If he sits and eats with you, fine. If he runs around, that is all right too because he has already eaten. Family togetherness can resume when Mark is a little older.

Second, you can stop snacks altogether an hour or two before dinner to permit Mark time to develop some appetite.

Then give him his dinner with you, but excuse him as soon as he loses interest or begins playing with his food. This should minimize any upset Mark's behavior might cause.

Third, move to the family room or living room for coffee and/or dessert. A change of place for dessert will shorten the time you spend at table, making it easier on Mark. At the same time it can provide a pleasant interlude for you and your husband.

You cannot make Mark behave like an older child; he is two years old. Your goal is not to change Mark but to find ways to make Mark's behavior compatible with the needs you and your husband have for a peaceful dinnertime.

# Toilet Training

**My first and only child is just two years old. He is not yet toilet trained. I want to train him in the easiest way. Some of my friends have been at it for months and they are very frustrated. I don't want this to happen to me.**

You have pinpointed the most essential element of successful toilet training, namely, that it is a normal learning experience for the growing child. Don't let it become a frustration for either of you.

Two conditions can keep toilet training simple. First, be sure the child is ready. Second, train the easy way.

We suggest four ways to determine readiness: (1) The child must be walking for some months before he is physically developed enough to be toilet trained. (2) Occasionally you should also find the child dry after a two-or-three-hour stretch. Extended periods of dryness indicate the child has some control over urination. (3) Since communication is a part of toilet training, it helps if the child is able to talk a bit. (4) Finally, the child around two often goes through an ornery period when *no* is the favorite word.

17

Common sense suggests you delay toilet training until such a period somewhat abates. Taken together, these factors indicate that the child will probably be ready for toilet training sometime between age two or three. Until that time do nothing about toilet training.

Once your child is ready, try this easy way to train in one week: Choose a five-day period (Monday through Friday) when both you and the child are feeling good and you have few other obligations. Get a child's potty which you can put in a room with a hard-surface floor, and where you plan to spend the morning. Remove the child's diapers, socks and shoes and let him run freely. Give water and juice liberally—and wait for nature. When the child starts to go or indicates he has to go, scoop him up gently and put him on the potty. Ignore any misses on the floor and praise and reward *anything* that gets in the potty.

One half day is long enough to be vigilant. In the afternoon put diapers back on and relax. Do the same thing each morning. By Thursday or Friday the child should be catching on. If so, continue extending the time he goes without diapers, and praise and reward all successes. If the child is not catching on, or if either of you is getting frustrated, quit. Wait a couple of months and try again. If a child is not toilet trained within five days, the cost in anxiety and frustration outweighs the benefit.

No harm is done in postponing toilet training for a few weeks or months. Great harm can be done by making it a heavy issue between you and your child. So toilet train the easy way both for your own sake and that of your child.

# Bed-Wetting

**Our son Jason has started to wet the bed at night. He is five years old now and he has been dry since he was two, so I know he can control himself. This couldn't have come at a**

worse time for us, since we have a new baby to care for. I've tried everything. We have yelled, been nice, ignored it—but nothing seems to work. Please help.

The return to wetting the bed in an older child is very common. Usually it is a reaction on the child's part to something new in the environment. In Jason's case, it may be related to the arrival of the new baby, or it may also reflect the very normal separation anxiety that a child experiences when beginning kindergarten.

Despite the strong possibility of social and/or psychological causes, you should first rule out a physical cause. If Jason is dry during the day, you can presume that the problem is not physical. On the other hand, if he wets regularly day and night or urinates frequently during the day, you should consult your physician.

The second step is a caution: Don't hassle him. Bed-wetting is common enough to be considered a normal reaction to life stress or the difficulties of growing up. A new baby, starting school, talk of divorce or moving to a new home are frequent culprits. Under stress the child reverts to an earlier form of behavior. If parents let him alone and are patient, the child is usually able within two to three weeks to return to his more mature ways.

Third, help him by making it easier for him to stay dry at night. While parents should not lecture or punish the child, they can take some practical measures to make it easier for him to last the night. Most obvious and important are restricting fluids after dinner and getting the child up to go to the bathroom just before the parents go to bed.

Let your child keep his self-respect during this period. Do not belittle or demean him by calling him a baby or making fun of him. Teach him to care for his wet pajamas and his sheets by himself. Rather than diapers, provide some extra-heavy training briefs covered with plastic pants which he can manage by himself and which will protect the bedding. In this way he maintains a feeling of control and can emerge from this difficulty with some measure of self-esteem.

Finally, if three weeks go by and the wetting still occurs half the time or more, you may want to provide an additional positive incentive. Set up a daily chart with smile faces for the times he is dry. Or drop a penny in a bottle on his dresser every night he is dry. Another good reward is to let him put his hand in a treasure jar every morning he is dry. The treasure jar contains folded slips of paper with mini-surprises written on them: a hug, a handful of peanuts, a toy car, a favorite activity, and so on. The important thing is that being dry is rewarded. Being wet receives silence, not even a lecture.

In summary: Check for a physical cause. Don't hassle or demean him. Take some practical steps to help him. And stay positive. Then allow some time for Jason to get back on the track, and you will succeed.

# Preparing for a New Baby

We are expecting our second child early in December. Our daughter Annie was three in July. She nurses once or twice a day and sleeps in our bed during the night. We are very close, rarely leaving her for more than an hour or two. In fact this second baby's birth will be the first "real separation." The doctor recommends a minimum one-day hospital stay.

What is the best preparation for Annie? Already people are saying, "You should have weaned her. You should leave her often, etc." I don't like this attitude, and we would value your opinion greatly.

To my mind you have expressed in concrete terms the best preparation you can give your daughter, namely, loving, supportive parenting. In the early years of life, support is expressed in tangible, physical ways. Parents are there. You can count on them. You can trust them, touch them, snuggle with them to fall asleep. Nothing is more important than the trust and security you convey to Annie with this attitude.

The usual criticism of such closeness is that the child will become shy and clinging and will remain babyish. Experienced parents find that this is simply not so. Secure infants become independent children. They are far more apt to get lost in the supermarket or set out for the park alone than to be forever clinging to mom.

I also disagree with the advice, "Leave Annie. Wean Annie." Raising young children by a timetable almost always backfires. "Little Johnny must be weaned before our vacation." "Little Sarah must be toilet-trained before Grandma visits." Little children cannot understand calendars, but they can understand their parents' moods. Even the best-intentioned parents communicate such desires to the child as demands.

Perhaps they express slight, almost imperceptible impatience. The child senses the demand and resists. When parents have no specific deadline, a child relaxes and easily progresses from baby behavior to more grown-up behavior.

Second, third or later children begin to go off from the family quite naturally, simply by tagging along with older brothers and sisters. With the first child, parents must take some initiatives. Now is a good time for you to start, not simply because a new baby is coming but, more importantly, because Annie is just about the right age to enjoy it.

You can find opportunities to expand her horizons. This is quite different from planning excuses to leave her. While threes do not yet play together very much, they do begin to enjoy being with other children. Try to get acquainted with other families with young children. Invite them over, visit them, go places together as families. Annie can begin to enjoy other children and adults in your company. Soon she is apt to request that she "go play with" another child.

As Annie begins to enjoy other children, you can leave her with a friend or neighbor while you do an errand or keep an appointment. You can then reciprocate and keep the friend's child. Such arrangements deepen neighborhood ties. When neighbors are close and enjoy each other's company, both parents and children profit. There is a world of difference between dumping children with neighbors or baby-sitters and introducing them to other warm, loving people.

Dad can be a tremendous help in preparing for a new baby. In a close family such as yours, Annie probably sees a lot of her dad already. As the arrival of the new baby draws closer, let dad invite Annie to go places and do things with him. It is easier to share mommy when dad is available for lots of activities.

With a child as young as Annie, you need not say much about the baby until its arrival is very near. Don't avoid the subject, but at the same time don't prepare Annie for months in advance. The subject won't really be interesting until the last couple of weeks.

Annie might get ready by making a gift for the new baby. At the same time you might buy or make something nice for Annie, so the new baby arrives home with a present for her.

Begin to broaden your contacts with other parents and children. But above all, continue the warm loving attitude you have already developed.

# Temper Tantrums

**My four-year-old likes to have temper tantrums when he knows I can't control him. Yesterday, in the toy department of a large store, he had a perfect kicking and screaming fit when I wouldn't buy him what he wanted. He will do this at home, too, but not as often. Mostly he puts on his show when I'm in a public place, and I get very embarrassed. Any**

**suggestions on how to handle these tantrums would be appreciated.**

Temper tantrums are common among preschool children. It is our job as parents to teach our children some self-control. We have some general "horse-sense" rules about temper tantrums which may be of some help.

1) For your own sake, avoid letting the tantrum occur in public places. If your child is prone to have tantrums while shopping, then don't take him shopping. Get a baby-sitter or leave him with a friend. If he does begin to carry on in a public place, pick him up and take him out to the car. Don't stay around to get embarrassed and then angry at him. Remove him from the scene.

2) Don't give in. It is important not to reward. You can be patient and let his anger run its course, but don't give him what he wants.

3) Protect him, yourself and anybody else from harm. Move him to a place where he can kick and thrash around without hurting anyone—or embarrassing you.

4) It is probably wise to avoid physical punishment. Some parents claim that a slap or a glass of cold water will shock a child out of a particular behavior. We are more inclined to let the temper run its course without any reward.

5) Ignore the tantrum as much as you can. Get him to a safe place. Protect everyone. Then let him unwind. Ignoring is more effective than punishing in the long run. Punishment can sometimes stop a behavior right now. But by ignoring you have a better chance to get rid of bad behavior for good.

6) Pay attention to other worthwhile behavior. If you can, try to distract him during the tantrum. Get him interested in doing something else. If not, wait until the tantrum is over and then get him involved in a worthwhile activity. This is far better than a lecture from you on why tantrums are not nice. It is better to teach your child what to do than what not to do.

# More Temper Tantrums

I am so upset with your advice on the four-year-old with temper tantrums. I agree with not rewarding the tantrum. But I feel your advice to ignore the tantrum couldn't be farther off-target.

When a child throws a tantrum he is deliberately challenging, mocking and defying the authority of the parent. To ignore this is to do the child a terrible injustice. I feel a child should definitely be spanked within the framework of love and affection.

We can easily agree with you that a child having a temper tantrum needs to be disciplined. We don't agree with you that he needs to be spanked. There are many ways to control or eliminate undesirable behavior such as temper tantrums. It is up to us as parents and disciplinarians to choose the best way.

Discipline is all the things we do as parents to shape the behavior of our children. Ignoring is one legitimate form of discipline. Ignoring does not mean permitting.

Basically, we are for whatever works best. Spanking can often have the advantage of getting rid of a certain behavior quickly and without paying too much attention to the problem behavior. If spanking works for you, then it may be a good discipline with your child.

Both research and practical experience, however, show that ignoring is the best way to eliminate behavior permanently. If the behavior can safely be ignored for a time, it is usually wiser to let the child have his tantrum and give him attention for some good behavior as soon as possible.

There are two kinds of temper tantrums, or rather there is a continuum between two poles. On one side is the "con job," where the child rather calculatingly throws a tantrum to get his way. On the other side, there is "beserk" behavior, where the child has clearly lost control. The situation in the letter you refer to was of the "con job" type.

With a "con job" tantrum, once the child is safe from harm and the parent safe from embarrassment, it is wisest to ignore the misbehavior. The child soon learns this is not an effective way to accomplish his goal. It doesn't work. Eventually, he will try some other way, and the parent begins to pay attention again.

With a "berserk" tantrum, the situation is different. The child has lost control of his own behavior and is flailing around, the helpless victim of his own rage. It would be cruel to let this kind of behavior go on for long. The object is to get through to the child in whatever way works. You might speak sharply to him, grab and hold him, insist he sit in a certain spot, spank him. The object is not to punish the child. The object is to interrupt a rage that is out of control. Only then can the rage be managed. A parent must try different techniques to find out what is most effective. Strange as it sounds, a two-year-old might respond to a command to "sit on the kitchen stool." The out-of-control rage is over.

The important thing is to control behavior. When you say the child has defied authority and must be spanked to indicate to him that you can control him, we think you are being one-dimensional. You are operating solely in the authoritative dimension. There are other ways to influence and change the actions of our children.

We are not advocating permissiveness. Children's behavior often needs boundaries set. We are saying quite simply that these boundaries do not always need to be set by edict or punishment. Behavior can be shaped in many ways.

# Sharing

**How do you get children to share? My three-year-old will share everything one day and nothing the next day. Even my five-year-old, who is often quite generous with his**

**things, sometimes refuses to share anything.**

How nice that you made positive statements about both your children. Your three-year-old shares sometimes, and your five-year-old is often generous. We parents are often so eager to have our children share that we notice only their shortcomings and fail to notice the positive things they are doing. Your comment indicates that you are aware of the positive side, even while you are concerned about the negative.

Sharing is one of those many behaviors in children that develops as the child grows. Two-year-olds simply cannot share. While they understand the word *mine* and use it often, they do not yet understand *yours*. Threes generally get a little more relaxed about their possessions and begin to share them, particularly when there are examples within the family. Sharing at this age is just beginning and is typically unpredictable.

As children see more and more examples of sharing within the family, and as other family members show pleasure over their sharing, the sharing gradually increases. Thus fours and fives display more and more generosity. Like all other behavior, sharing does not proceed with perfect smoothness. On a bad day any child can revert to possessive behavior and refuse to share.

Unfortunately for parents, social pressure often dictates that children share even from the earliest years. Parents may feel the disapproval of relatives or friends when a two-year-old refuses to share her toys. Then parents try to force the child to share. Forced sharing is a contradiction in terms. Tears or even tantrums usually follow. It calls for a lot of social skill on the part of parents to handle the situation without forcing the child beyond his capabilities. The social skills of a young child are slight. It is up to you as a parent to recognize the child's inability to share and at the same time not antagonize friends or neighbors. Use a little humor, and above all try to keep the event from becoming a big issue.

There are some positive steps you can take to avoid battles among children. We find that each toy should clearly belong to a specific child. The fewer "family toys" the better. The owner may play with a toy at any time for as long as he pleases. Others may play when the owner permits. When children in the family are close in age, it is often better to buy two identical toys than two different toys. When a child knows clearly that some things really belong to her, she can share more easily than the child who owns nothing and therefore must cling to everything. This means that parents must support ownership rather than threaten it in the early years.

A few items should be protected by parents. Even adults reserve some things for themselves. Mom rarely shares a valuable piece of jewelry. Dad probably wouldn't loan his new car. Similarly, with children, security items like blankets or favorite Teddy bears should be absolutely reserved. New birthday presents are often too dear to share immediately. Again a parent can tactfully run interference and let the child be possessive about a new Big Wheel for a day or two. After that the child himself will probably share it.

In general, protect the child who is not ready to share, praise the child who does share, and ignore or treat lightly the failures to share. Do this and your child's generosity will grow.

# Letting Children Help

I have two preschool children who are just beginning to help around the house. Could you suggest some jobs that young children can do and some ways to get them to be helpful?

Learning to work is important for children. It not only

contributes to the running of the household but, more importantly, it gives children a good self-image, a sense of being capable, independent persons.

Children strive for competence. Almost from the time they can talk, they declare, "I wanna do it myself." From about the age of three, children can learn to do simple jobs which satisfy this urge for independence.

The famous educator of the young child, Maria Montessori, incorporated "lessons in practical life" into her education of the preschooler. These "lessons" were nothing more nor less than cleaning, food preparation, personal grooming and similar necessities. Her principles are helpful to the mother working with her own child, and we are indebted to her for many of the following ideas:

1) Teach children to do real jobs. Do not *pretend* they are working. Do not hover over them or redo the job as soon as they are out of sight. Such behavior is demeaning to their dignity as capable persons. Instead, select a job within the child's capability.

2) Simplify jobs to bring them within the child's capability. Bed-making, for example, can be made easy: Use a contour sheet on the mattress and, on top, a quilt or comforter. No top sheet, blanket or bedspread is necessary. The comforter serves all functions. In the morning the child straightens the comforter neatly on the bed, and the bed is made. With this method, a child can learn to make his bed around the age of four. Use your ingenuity to apply this principle of simplifying to other tasks.

3) Whenever possible, build in aids to help the child do a job independently. For example, when a child is learning to set the table, use a paper placemat on which you draw each part of the table setting. Using this model the child can correctly set each place at the table independently.

A real drawback to independence in the kitchen is that all counters and appliances are scaled for adult size. Get a sturdy, non-tipping step stool, light enough for the child to move around by himself, thus permitting him to work at the sink or stove.

4) Teach a new job by demonstrating each step carefully. Montessori insisted that her teachers practice a task over and over, step-by-step, in order to demonstrate it correctly to young children. In teaching a job, use a minimum of words, but demonstrate the action clearly. The child will learn by imitating your actions.

While young children love to "help mommy," they usually need mommy working right beside them. Although their actual helpfulness at this age may seem slight, do not ignore or refuse them. Give your child every opportunity to help, and he or she will work more and more independently as time goes by.

Specific jobs that preschool children can do include dusting, bed-making, and setting and clearing the table. Shining shoes and polishing silver are jobs which four- and five-year-olds love to do. Since water is popular with preschoolers, washing dishes or painted furniture is another possibility. Again, select a job within the child's capability and demonstrate exactly how to do it including getting out and putting away equipment.

Primary school children can also learn to sweep and vacuum and clean the bathroom. Again demonstrate each job clearly.

Picking up clutter is an endless job in households with young children. Preschool and primary school age children can be genuinely helpful here. If, however, you place a young child in a totally cluttered room with the instructions, "Pick up this mess," she is almost certain to be overwhelmed. (Aren't you?) Help your child by breaking the task down into manageable jobs and assigning them one at a time: "Ellen, you pick up the dolls and doll clothes and put them in this box. Jamie, you get all the plastic animals and men and put them in this box." Step-by-step the task does get finished.

Many steps in food preparation can be shared by young

children. Scrubbing vegetables is popular, and children can help with slicing and grating. Three- and four-year-olds might slice bananas using a table knife. Six- and seven-year-olds can learn to use a paring knife. As always, select a slicing task which is not too difficult and demonstrate the safe way to cut.

When your child learns to do a task correctly, be sure to notice and praise his efforts. Be appreciative. Capable children are a genuine help. And they are making important strides in growing up. In helping your children become competent and independent, you are performing one of your most important tasks as a parent.

# Masturbation

**My five-year-old daughter masturbates. This has been an off-and-on occurrence since she was about three. All the secular childrearing books say this is perfectly normal and to merely instruct the child to do this in private since some people will find the practice embarrassing. Isn't there something more Christian and caring to say and do?**

Thank you for asking so directly about a matter which is very common but which nobody wants to mention. Children do touch their genitals with some frequency, and adults find this behavior embarrassing. What to do?

You ask for "something more Christian and caring to say and do" than to tell your child that private masturbation is all right. Do not overlook the fact that values toward sexuality can be communicated in many ways. Hugging and touching your child is a positive way to say that bodies can express affection, a valuable message which both dad and mom can communicate to boys as well as girls. Through such behavior you can begin to express your own values about physical love even with young children.

To answer your question more directly, let us suggest two extremes which are best avoided. As children many of us were told that any unnecessary attention to a private part of the body was seriously sinful. Such a negative introduction to sexuality is unfortunate. The other extreme is to tell the child that masturbation is a normal and healthy part of growing up. Most parents take a position between these two extremes.

Most parents want to say that sex is a beautiful aspect of life, *but* don't do it now. As a result most parents try to stop the masturbation while saying nothing. The message to the child may well be that sex is a matter that cannot be discussed.

In other words, parents want to give a double message: Your body is nice, but don't play with it at this time. So we should say just that. The clear and spoken double message will be less confusing to the child than a half-silence.

Personally we oppose hypocrisy. What is unacceptable in public is also unacceptable in private. We would simply tell our child that it is not acceptable to put her hand on her genitals even though her genitals feel good and are a beautiful part of her.

You must distinguish between your values and your strategy. Our parental value is that we do not wish our child at age five to masturbate in public or in private. Our strategy would involve two parts. First, we would give the "nice-but-not-now" message directly in order to cause as little confusion as possible. Second, in order to be effective and to avoid undue emphasis on the entire issue, we would for the most part ignore her behavior.

Ignoring is not doing nothing. In fact, ignoring is the best way to stop a specific behavior permanently. Masturbation in a five-year-old is not all that serious. We would treat it like sex words (shockers) in a seven-year-old. A rather firm admonition, "Don't do that," and, then, let it alone.

Masturbation, like sex words, is not a sign of eventual corruption and dissolution. Rather it is a fairly normal attempt to explore the body, one that, with reasonable parental help, a child will outgrow.

A heavy-handed parental attempt to wipe out this activity now and forever may have unfortunate implications for the child's self-image. She needs to know her body and her genitals are God's creation. They are not dirty, and the pleasures are not sinful. On the other hand, the parent can tell the child rather directly to "stop it" without ruining the child's future sex life.

To sum up: A parent can legitimately tell the child to stop masturbating in public and in private. Once the message has been given, don't dwell on the behavior. Finally, keep the whole issue in perspective: troublesome, yes; weighty, no.

# Preschool — When and Where?

**I am the mother of a two-year-old boy and a newborn baby. I am thinking about sending my older child to nursery school. At what age is a child ready for nursery school? How do you pick a good one?**

Nursery school combines learning and play experience for children three to five. It offers opportunity for social and intellectual development. Children usually attend nursery school for a two- or three-hour period, from one to five days a week.

Nursery school is not baby-sitting or day care. Many nursery school teachers have studied early childhood education and have extensive first-hand experience with children.

Many educators of preschool children recommend nursery school starting at age three. We recommend, however, that the decision be made on an individual basis by those who know the child best, the parents.

The child is ready for nursery school when he or she is:
a) interested in the outside world; b) ready to tackle it.

Interest in the outside world is often indicated by its
opposite: boredom at home. If the preschooler frequently
grows tired of her toys, constantly looks for something to do
and someone to play with, then she may well profit from
nursery school. The child is ready when she shows an
attraction to outsiders, approaches new experiences with
confidence and enthusiasm. Many three-year-old children are
rather retiring and quite happy with the activities at home.
At four, this same child becomes outgoing, boisterous and
bored.

Keep in mind that first-time parents frequently think
their child is ready for experiences too soon. They enroll their
children in programs at the minimum ages, complaining that
program directors were blind to the fact that their child was
ready months earlier.

Parents of later children, however, are apt to delay entry
into school. They know that a child need not do everything
this year. Next year might be even better.

You can find out about nursery schools in several ways.
Visit the school; observe the children; talk with the teacher.
Ask others who have sent children to the school.

Most nursery schools are glad to let parents observe the
class, which is the best way to gain an impression. (Leave
your children with a friend when you go. You want to disrupt
the school's normal procedure as little as possible.)

Notice the number of children in the class. Eight or 10
children is comfortable for a single teacher with no helpers.
Fifteen or so is the maximum a single teacher can handle
effectively.

Observe the kind and amount of equipment. Will the
equipment be interesting and challenging to your child? Is
there enough? Is it different from what he has at home?

Observe the amount of play space. Do the children have

ample opportunity to move around? Or do they appear restless from too much sitting still? Above all, does the balance seem suited to the energy level of your child?

How does the teacher relate to the children? Is she warm and enthusiastic? Does she control the class effectively without being too harsh or too casual? Does she encourage learning activities, neither pushing too hard nor being indifferent to the child's achievements? Do the children seem happy?

No school or teacher will conform perfectly to your preferences. Use these questions as guidelines not as standards of perfection.

Finally, talk about your decision with friends who have sent children to nursery school and whose opinions you value. They can help you decide where and when to send your child.

# Successful Birthday Parties

Last year I gave a birthday party for my five-year-old daughter. She was very excited about it, but during the party she tried to boss all the children and by the time I served refreshments she broke down and cried. I would appreciate any suggestions you have for a more successful party this year.

Your daughter's crying indicates how successful the party was. She was probably so thrilled about her big day that the festivities finally overwhelmed her. Such behavior is not unusual.

This year plan to control the excitement by setting limits: First, limit the time she must anticipate her party. Make a guest list and send out invitations only three or four days in advance. Next, limit the number of guests. An old and wise rule-of-thumb for children's parties is to invite the same number of guests as the age of your child. Third, limit the length of the party to two hours maximum. To make certain it ends on time, drive the children home yourself. Finally, limit the vigorous, stimulating physical games by alternating them with quieter activities such as opening presents and eating.

In planning the party, devote your efforts to details which are important to children rather than details which please adults. Adults plan guest lists to repay social obligations. They serve unusual foods as a special treat. They plan beautiful table settings on a single theme cleverly carried out. None of these details are important to children.

When selecting guests choose children your daughter wants, not children of your friends or relatives. Your two-year-old niece need not be invited simply because she is family. Invite relatives another time.

Children prefer food which is simple and familiar. Skip the special new sandwich filling in favor of peanut butter and jelly, hamburgers, hot dogs or whatever is the favorite choice. Consult your daughter about the menu. She is an expert on six-year-old eating behavior.

The cake need not be a decorated masterpiece on which you spend hours, but it should be special in some way. An ordinary cake cut into a special shape or a square cake topped with a tic-tac-toe design (use small chocolate candies) are examples of simple details which are received with enthusiasm.

Arrange for lots of small prizes and lots of game winners. Individually-wrapped candies, sticks of gum, pennies and small plastic animals or trinkets can be mixed together in a large prize dish. Winners choose after every game. Offering many prizes and many chances to win almost insures that everyone will win a few times. To be certain that everyone wins, offer a consolation prize from time to time.

Another way to make everyone a winner is to offer door prizes. Each guest (including the birthday girl) has a number written on her hand with marking pencil as she arrives. Call numbers from time to time throughout the party. Winners get to choose a door prize in the order called, but everyone is called eventually.

As children get older, they can better tolerate excitement. Your daughter probably will not repeat the tearful episode of last year. But do not expect her best behavior during the party. Try to ignore a little bossiness or temperament. Concentrate on food, games and prizes that little girls like, and you will have a fast-moving party that all will enjoy.

# Keeping Up With Four-Year-Olds

I know parents always wish they had as much energy as their children, but in my case this is no joke. My youngest child is a four-year-old boy. Although we have other children who are now in school, we have never had one with an energy level like this one. He moves and talks constantly. He is happy enough, I think, but I am afraid I will either squelch him too much or wear myself out trying to keep up with him. Any suggestions?

As most of us know, people have many different personalities, shy or outgoing, quiet or boisterous, commanding or retiring. Many years ago the researchers at the Gesell Institute pointed out that children, in addition to having different individual personalities, also go through personality cycles. In general (we can never assign exact ages because people vary), threes are rather retiring and prefer to stay close to the parent, fives are eager to please adults. And fours? Well, fours are about as you describe your son.

Four-year-olds are typically loud, brash, confident. The child who at three was shy and retiring, at four can take on the world. A four-year-old will try such quirky behavior as kicking a total stranger just to see what reaction he gets. (We admit, regretfully, we draw that example from one of our own four-year-olds.) Apparently what you are experiencing just now is a naturally active, extroverted child at a particularly brash age.

What can you do? First, schedule plenty of time for vigorous outdoor play. This is no hothouse plant. Get him outside every day.

Second, watch his diet. There is much controversy over how diet and behavior are related, so you might observe for yourself. Some parents notice increased activity after high doses of sugar. Watch particularly for treats with lots of refined sugar and soft drinks with sugar, artificial sweeteners and/or caffeine. Whatever your child's activity level, you cannot go wrong by avoiding these items.

Third, try some out-of-the-home stimulation and amusement in the form of library story hours, a church preschool class, or a nursery school. We personally feel that the high-activity, "I-can-lick-the-world" behavior of fours is one way they tell us they are ready to meet the world outside the home.

Fourth, arrange play sessions with other children instead of, or in addition to, nursery school. Fours are usually sociable and love to have friends over to play. Your arrangements can be spontaneous or systematic. You might arrange with one or two other mothers to alternate play sessions on a regular basis. You do not need a degree in preschool education to play host to two or three four-year-olds, just enough time and energy to supervise, provide toys and feed them.

Unfortunately we cannot bottle the energy of four-year-olds, but we can rejoice in their good health and good spirit.

# Treating Hyperactivity

**We have a four-year-old son who is into everything. He**

can't sit still, and he is a terror around the house. He talks constantly, teases his two sisters, accidentally breaks almost all his toys, and is slowly driving me crazy. My neighbor says he is hyperactive and that I should see my physician. What do you think?

The word *hyperactive* has two meanings, one very general and one a specific medical diagnosis. In general, *hyperactive* means "overly active." Your son is certainly that. It sounds as though you have your hands full.

Medically, *hyperactive* refers to uncontrolled behavior due to a physical, neurological problem. Nerve impulses are not adequately controlled. The child is unable to learn in school or to perform athletically because he cannot control his energy.

The treatment possibilities can be summarized by the three D's: drugs, diet and discipline.

If the problem is physical, the child may well respond to *drugs* like Ritalin or Cylert. Although these drugs would "speed up" an adult, they serve to control the unchecked nerve impulses of a hyperactive child. These drugs take effect within a few hours. If the hyperactivity is physically caused, you will know within 24 to 48 hours because your child will be noticeably calmer with the drugs.

Tranquilizers have also been used with some success to treat hyperactivity in children. Valium is perhaps the most common one. Drugs, however, should be used as a last resort, and only where the problem has been shown to be physically based. Drugs have too many bad side effects. They also have the danger of masking other problems.

*Diet* is certainly a far safer way to begin treating hyperactivity than drugs. In some cases change in diet works; in other cases it doesn't.

Dr. Ben Feingold in his book *Why Your Child Is Hyperactive* (Random House, 1974) recommends eliminating all foods with synthetic food coloring, flavoring and additives.

Other allergists systematically eliminate certain foods such as dairy products, chocolate and refined sugar. They find that when certain of these foods are eliminated, the hyperactive child improves.

In any case, finding the culprits in diet requires detective-like observation on your part. If you are fortunate enough to find a physician who works with diet and hyperactivity, you will have a helpful advisor in a complicated situation.

*Discipline* is the least radical and most difficult approach of the three. It takes parental time and attention to discipline well. Good discipline requires consistency and follow-through. The parent cannot say something and then fail to enforce it. For this reason, good discipline usually does not try to cover everything. Rather, parents select those few areas which are most important to them and where they feel they can be most effective. A lot of growing-up behavior (running, spilling, noise, etc.) can be ignored.

Good discipline requires that at least as much time be spent in rewarding good behavior as in punishing bad. Let me give a few simple suggestions on how you might apply these principles to your son.

You might begin by selecting one behavior he does well and one that you feel he must stop. Discuss these with your husband. Be very certain what behavior it is you wish to encourage and what behavior you wish to stop. Also, agree what you will use as a reward and what will be the penalty. Don't try to do too much.

Let us suppose you feel you must begin by stopping his teasing and bullying of his sisters. When he teases, tell him firmly to stop. If the teasing is still going on 60 seconds later, physically remove him from the scene. Set him in a chair. If he won't stay, sit on him. Make him stay just long enough for the bad behavior to stop. (Even a minute or two can seem like an eternity to an overactive child.) Then let him go again.

What to reward? With all that energy, he must be doing

something good. Suggest that he pick up the living room daily, and reward him with your attention. Let him talk into a tape recorder for five minutes and then hear himself. Even more simply, if he likes to talk, take time to talk to him. Talking is certainly a valued skill, as any parent whose child is late to talk will be quick to tell you.

You have a real task with your four-year-old. In dealing with him, try discipline and diet. If that does not work, see your physician about the possibility of using drugs.

# Curiosity About Sex

**Recently the four-year-old neighbor boy asked my three-year-old to pull down her panties. My daughter told me about it. I have not yet talked to the boy's mother. What can I do to insure that this does not happen again and does not get worse as the children get older?**

In little children curiosity about the opposite sex is just that—curiosity. Around age three a boy learns that he will grow into a man, and his sex will not change. Girls learn the same thing about being female. Apparently this learning is tied to development since it occurs in all cultures, cannot be grasped before age three, and is understood even though no one formally explains these facts to the child.

In their conversation three-year-olds give many cues about their newfound understanding: "Mommy's a girl." "Daddy's a boy." "Brother is a boy." These and similar remarks dot their conversation.

With the arrival of this important new knowledge, curiosity about their own sex and the opposite sex naturally follows. The child is simply expressing a desire to know what the opposite sex looks like.

The child's curiosity does not "get worse" as the years progress. Once satisfied, it subsides.

40

Frequently a baby brother or sister arrives around this time, and the curiosity of the three-year-old is conveniently satisfied. Apparently your neighbor boy was not so fortunate.

What should you do? Tell your daughter not to pull down her panties outside. Do this in the same way you would teach her not to pick her nose or stuff food in her mouth. That is, teach her that this is a convention we observe, neither more nor less serious than other conventions.

You might be watchful when the children play together. Should the boy repeat his request, discourage him in the same manner you would discourage other unacceptable behavior. For example, "Hey, Scott, I don't want you to do that anymore." Such a remark from you should be sufficient.

Should you talk to the mother? If you think she will become very upset, break off a friendship, punish her child severely, or forbid him to play in your yard, do not even mention it. The matter is not serious enough to warrant such consequences. If you think she can help you watch the children and casually and gently discourage the undesirable behavior, tell her.

Above all, remember that curious children are not manifesting an unhealthy interest in sex. Rather they are expressing their new knowledge about a wonderful fact of creation—that God made us male and female.

# Readiness for Kindergarten?

My first child will soon be old enough for kindergarten. She is very apprehensive, however, with new people and new situations, and she doesn't want me to leave her sight. This is not a family characteristic, as her younger brother, age three, willingly goes off with other people. Since I can't accompany her to kindergarten each day, what should I do?

The first point, which is clear from your letter, is that

children do have very different attitudes and personalities, even within the same family. Your daughter is apt to remain somewhat shy and your son rather outgoing. Let us accept and welcome these differences in people.

When shyness interferes with normal functioning, however, the child needs some encouragement. What occasionally happens is that a two- or three-year-old has some genuine fears. At this age mother stays close to the child as a comfort and support. Then, around age four, children usually become more noisy, boisterous and outgoing, almost as a signal that they are ready to tackle the larger world outside the family. Certain children, however, choose to continue the more fearful behavior. Perhaps mom is supporting them in the same way she did when they were two or three. Support for children is part of parenting. The challenge in this case is to support the shy child, but to support her as a four- or five-year-old, not as a two-year-old.

As we get older, life makes more demands on us. Now life (mother? society?) demands that your little girl do some things on her own. Take this attitude and look for opportunities for separations that are brief and pleasant. Choose someone such as a relative or a close, friendly neighbor and plan to leave your daughter there for a period of only 10 minutes.

"Angie, mom has to pick up the dry cleaning and you're going to stay with Mrs. Tucker. I'll only be gone a few minutes."

"I wanna come."

"Not this time, but you can come when I go grocery shopping."

Just give a matter-of-fact statement. Then leave her, do your errand, and be back in no more than 10 minutes. Praise her moderately if she enjoys herself; be moderately sympathetic if she was unhappy. In general, try to convey the attitude that this is not a big deal.

Note that this attitude is different from the handling of a

two-year-old. At two the child cannot understand time. Either mother is there or she isn't. You can leave your four- or five-year-old with an explanation because at this age she understands, at least dimly, that mother promised to come back in a few minutes and she kept her word.

Continue leaving your little girl in pleasant situations. Always be matter-of-fact. As she gets used to the idea, you can lengthen the activities. Can she go alone to a preschool class at your church or library? Invite other children over as often as possible and welcome opportunities for your daughter to visit.

Never scold or shame her for being scared or babyish. Stick to your matter-of-fact attitude: "Sometimes we do things with mommy. Sometimes we do things without mommy. Life is like that."

Finally, give your daughter time. If she is really fearful of kindergarten, why not try nursery school for one year? The individual readiness of each child is far more important than the fact that the child is five. Once she realizes that there are many good people and pleasant experiences awaiting her outside the family, she will be ready to tackle and enjoy kindergarten and the years beyond.

# Finding a Good Baby-Sitter

I have to go back to work soon. We are short of cash and, really, I have no choice. I have a boy three and a girl 14 months old. I need to know how to find a good baby-sitter. What kind of questions should I ask? I want a baby-sitter that will be good to my children. I don't want them scared or hit or anything abusive. The children are already used to being away from us at times. But I'm having a hard time finding a permanent baby-sitter that I can really trust.

This question is becoming increasingly common in our world

today. Strange that in the most affluent nation on earth more and more families need two incomes just to survive. Since baby-sitters are hard to find, many settle for anyone who agrees to do the job. Obviously you care too much to take such a course.

Child abuse has been uncovered even in baby-sitters provided by licensed agencies. Your concern is real. The great difficulty is that adults who appear quite competent with other adults sometimes act very differently when with small children. Little children can try an adult's patience in the extreme and, when upset, some adults respond with rage, punishment and abuse. For these reasons I doubt that even a careful interview would disclose the personality of the person you wish to hire.

What to do? We think the safest course is to seek recommendations through people you know personally. Ask your friends whom they have used. Look for someone who is used to small children, since baby-sitting school-age children is quite different from baby-sitting young children.

If your immediate friends cannot help you, you might contact other working mothers through a women's club or church group. Perhaps you can locate two or three other mothers in a situation similar to yours. You might then arrange for one mother to baby-sit all the children. Financially it might be as lucrative for her as working.

Another possibility is to seek out a mother whose last child is a preschooler. When a family has school age children, the last child often gets bored at home alone. Such a mother might take your children to earn a little extra income and to provide companionship for her own child. You can judge how she will mother your children by how she mothers her own.

Can you get by on a part-time job? If so, you might locate another mother in a situation like yours and try to find two part-time jobs or one shared job. Each of you works half the time on the job and cares for both sets of children the other half.

The advantages of such a solution are many. Your half-time income goes farther because you pay nothing for baby-sitting. You are also able to spend more time with your children. Your baby-sitter is someone who is just as concerned as you about the welfare of the children. In a shared job even the employer benefits because, in the case of sickness, it is easier to make arrangements to cover the job with two adults than with one.

A shared job is impossible to find, you say? Difficult, yes; impossible, no. Employers would rather train one person than two. If the job does not require extensive training, however, this is not a serious objection. Fringe benefits such as insurance, pensions and vacations are more difficult to allocate. Here we must ask where our priorities lie. What is more important, an employer's record book or the welfare of our children? Do jobs exist to benefit people, or do people exist for jobs?

More and more parents need extra income and good care for children. Shared jobs are a means to provide both on a personal family-to-family basis. If enough parents demand such work conditions, business will begin to listen.

# Facing Death

**No one in our immediate family has died recently, so our preschool-age children have never been to a funeral home or to a burial. Should I take the children along when I visit a funeral home even though they have no particular relationship with the deceased? How young is too young for children to face death?**

Death is a natural part of life. To avoid the mention of death, even with children, is impossible.

Our basic principle is to treat death as natural and normal. We can celebrate death, or we can fear it. We can

45

welcome it or fight it. But all of us, young and old, must learn to accept death. It is the way people and other living creatures leave this life.

Children can go with their parents to wakes and cemeteries. Why not? The family goes, and they go along. To keep them home would suggest that death is too difficult a fact for them to face. In fact, children are generally less upset by death than adults.

Children might well go to wakes where they do not particularly know the deceased. Children can thus get used to the idea of death without feeling the loss of someone dear and important.

We take children to wakes and cemeteries as the opportunities arise regardless of age. Wakes and cemeteries are probably inconsequential for two- and three-year-olds, and for that very reason, it is an opportune time to begin to take them.

Children may object to going because they are bored or afraid. If they object strongly, I would not force them. Ask them again next time.

When you take preschool children to wakes and burials, expect them to act their age. They are apt to be noisy, to laugh at the wrong time and to want to run around. They may wish to touch the corpse. They may ask questions like, "Does she have legs?"

Rather than overwhelm them with the solemnity of death, it is best to let them act their age. Don't be too hard on them. If you bring small children, plan to pay your respects briefly and then leave.

Most important of all in death education, however, is the "hidden agenda." Your children are bound to hear your own gut feelings whether you voice them or not. What is the unspoken message you give them about death?

Get in touch with yourself and try to be honest with your children. Are you afraid? Let them know that. Children understand fear. Are you sad? Don't hide your tears.

Even with our faith, death remains a great mystery. Admit that. There is no need to try to make up answers nor to sugarcoat a hard fact.

Don't tell children anything you yourself don't believe. Don't say dead people are with angels unless you have a firm belief that this is so. The answer to death is not a belief in details about the afterlife. The answer lies in trust in the Lord and in the experience of fellowship and love mobilized by family and friends.

Children need to learn about death from the earliest age. They learn best by being with their parents when death is faced.

# Six to Twelve
# Grade-Schoolers

The elementary school years have been called a period of latency, a quiet time when gains are consolidated and formal learning is begun. Problems arise nevertheless—like fighting, teasing, lying, stealing and sassing. Also of concern to parents are school problems, dawdling over homework, piano lessons, junk food, and how much to give for allowances. Children want to stay overnight with their friends. Television programs need to be monitored. Family chores need to be initiated and organized. Children should learn the beauty of sex from their parents. All these issues and many more provide the theme for parent-child interaction during the grade school and preteen years.

# Lying

Why do children lie? My six-year-old has started telling "whoppers." Most of them seem harmless, but I worry that he will get into the habit of thinking that truth doesn't matter. How do I get him to stop?

Lying or, perhaps better, playing around with the truth is very common from ages five to eight for three reasons.

Fantasy may be the biggest reason. Children at this age still live in a wonderful world of dream and myth where the truth is larger than any mere person, place or thing. To make life more interesting, the child invents or creates an adventure, then tells it as a real event. Dr. Seuss described this tendency beautifully in his book *And to Think That I Saw It on Mulberry Street.*

Sometimes parents worry that, unless they correct their child, he will grow up unable to distinguish between fantasy and reality. This is unlikely, and if it occurs, it will be for reasons other than the failure of parents to point out reality. All of us, including six-year-olds, receive plenty of examples each day that help us distinguish between what is real and what is imagined.

Frankly, we are more worried about the parent who has lost the ability to imagine. We poor parents are so beaten down by everyday events that we long ago lost the facility to live out imaginary fantasy adventures. A wise parent may join his child in a fantasy story for a time, create events back and forth, then gently lead the child back to the less interesting real world.

A second reason that truth is stretched at this age may be to gain attention. Here the focus is not so much on fun and whimsy as it is on showing off or shocking. The child may present himself as having accomplished some marvelous task or having met famous people. To shock, the child may bring home stories of horror or tragedy that prove inaccurate.

Getting the attention of others is a reasonable desire for anyone. We all like to attract notice. There are, however, many better ways to attract attention than presenting imaginary achievements to others. Since the "lie" in such an "attention-getting" case is annoying but harmless, we would suggest ignoring it.

Some parents feel that such ignoring is being permissive. They want an authoritative confrontation. Actually, ignoring is the discipline of choice here. If the child "lies" to gain attention, don't give it to him. Don't even give him an explanation of the difference between real and imaginary. Nothing. Go on to some other topic.

Finally, children may lie to avoid trouble and to keep from getting caught. This tactic is more common with older children. At least we adults understand the motivation behind this kind of lying. The child is protecting his or her self-interest, a move we dislike because it is calculated and deliberate.

The best way to stop this type of untruth is not to ask questions that require self-incrimination. Our legal system protects adults from being forced to admit their crimes. We parents can offer the same privilege to our children. Gather the evidence from other sources. Confront, accuse and punish children when necessary. But don't force them to tell on themselves.

This eliminates big battles about confessing and telling the truth. The parent no longer has to demand that the child confess, with dire threats if he does not or if he lies. It avoids giving too much attention to misbehavior and, at the same time, provides no temptation for the child to lie.

# Shyness

**My daughter, who is seven and in second grade, is very shy. She is lively and talkative around home, but at school or**

with any group of children or adults outside the home she is quiet and seems to find it difficult to join in the group. How can I help her?

While human behavior is too complex to explain by a simple cause-and-effect solution, there are some factors which might contribute to shyness in a child. A child may be shy simply because he or she has had little experience with people. For children in our modern nuclear family, mother is often the child's constant companion through the preschool years. Mother may become the almost exclusive companion. Sometimes this can scarcely be helped if there are no relatives nearby or no children of a similar age in the neighborhood. Perhaps mother is somewhat shy herself and does not do much visiting in the neighborhood. Whatever the reason, the child does not see many people outside the few members of the immediate family.

Mother's presence is important during the child's early years; having mother present, however, does not mean excluding everyone except mother. We think the ideal social situation for a child is to have a mother who is present and supportive throughout the preschool years, a father who enjoys being with his family, and a wide range of people from outside the family whom the child meets and enjoys within the security of her own home.

Another possible reason for shyness is criticism or "put-downs." Perhaps one of the parents tends to be critical of the child's efforts. Sometimes relatives or baby-sitters have expectations of a child beyond what is normal for the child's age and capabilities. Even preteens or teenage brothers or sisters can be severe critics at times. If these people exert a strong influence on the child, she may draw back in fear of criticism.

If you think your child is being criticized, you might make a real effort to give the child positive support. Such support must be tactful and genuine. Even a seven-year-old can recognize phoniness and will suspect hypocrisy if you suddenly start praising her for everything. Make a list for yourself of the things your child does well. The very act of defining and writing down her strong points will make you more aware of them, and you will be more apt to notice and praise them.

If you feel she has been somewhat isolated from people outside the family, you can try to find ways to broaden your family. Let her invite friends over often, not just occasionally. If she is comfortable with one friend but uncomfortable with a group, you can gradually introduce her to groups. Have very informal parties from time to time. Three or four girls might gather to make masks or costumes. By having a planned activity and keeping the time short, you take away any pressure on your daughter to play hostess.

Adults, too, can expand your family. Could you hire a teenage girl to come in to help you in some way? Could you plan outings with another family so that both children and adults come together? Sometimes an occasion even arises for someone outside your family to live with you, probably on a temporary basis. Such an arrangement can be an opportunity rather than a burden for your family.

In dealing with other people you can gradually and gently stretch her capabilities. Can she go to the store all by herself? Can she face the librarian with an overdue library book all by herself? Can she attend a matinee at the movie with another friend without any adult along? Each time she tries a new task, support her with your confidence that she can do it. If a new task is too overwhelming, let her take one step at a time. You take her to the store, but she makes a purchase.

Your child is probably going to remain somewhat shy. It is doubtful that you could or would want to bring about a complete personality change. A world full of extroverts would be a very noisy place. By communicating your support and approval of your daughter, you can help her become *attractively* shy rather than *uncomfortably* shy.

# Shoplifting

**Our 10-year-old son was caught stealing several magazines at the local store. This is the second time. The store manager gave him a talking to and called us. He told us we had better do something about our son. What can we do? He has not been in any other trouble.**

Shoplifting occurs in 50 percent or more of preadolescent youngsters. An incident or two does not mean that your child is set on a course leading to a life of crime. It does give you as parents an early opportunity to set your child straight on an important aspect of getting along in society.

Why do small children shoplift? The most common reason seems to be the dare, a chance to test their limits against adult wits. "I dare you to take it!" is an oft-heard child challenge.

Another common reason is the materialistic greed which pervades our society from top to bottom. The child takes something he wants and cannot obtain in any other way.

The reasons for shoplifting may be interesting, but this is not the time for rational explanations and discourses on the moral order. This is the time to come down hard. This is the time for shock tactics.

Psychologist Lawrence Kohlberg tells us that 10-year-olds are not very sensitive to the feelings of others and do not act to protect the rights of others. They do, however, understand that their behavior has *consequences*. They can learn from consequences. Parents must let the shoplifter experience these consequences.

A firm lecture from the store owner or a warning from the police about what will happen if the behavior is repeated is very effective. When such shock tactics are used before stealing has become a habit, research indicates that, in the great majority of cases, the stealing never occurs again.

Of course the child must return the stolen items or pay for them. Restitution is another important consequence that the child must face. We would accompany our child in a visit to the store owner to arrange restitution.

After the stern lecture by the store owner and/or police, and after restitution has been made, then forget it. The matter is closed. The child made a mistake. He paid the price. Time now to get on with life. Parental reminders, verbalized suspicion, continued questions about stealing, and checking the child's room provide too much attention for behavior that needs to disappear. In most cases the shock tactic will be sufficient to eliminate the stealing, and continued nagging may only bring it back.

# Teasing

**We have a 12-year-old daughter, a five-year-old son and two other children. The girl teases the younger brother unmercifully. I know teasing happens in most families, so we have tried to ignore it. The younger boy is almost always upset, however, and their carrying-on drives the rest of us crazy.**

Sometimes brothers and sisters go through stages when they can barely be in the same room with each other. The situation may last for a few months or for years. These stages pass, and the children frequently become friends (or at least stop being enemies) after a time. The fact that it will pass, however, is little help to you now.

You are right to try to ignore the teasing behavior. Ignoring, however, is only part of the solution. You can try two other approaches: Change the home environment in certain ways and pay attention to the 12-year-old for the good things she does rather than the teasing.

Your first task in trying to change the home environment is to observe closely for a few days. Find out what situations lead to the most teasing. You will probably discover that certain times are worse than others. Watching television, doing chores together, riding in the car, and any pre-mealtime periods when children are hungry and cross are examples of some problem times.

Next, plan ways to separate the combatants at the problem times. Supervise television so that 12-year-olds and five-year-olds watch different programs. Assign seating in the car so that the children are at least out of touching range if not vocal range. Do not explain to the children that you are separating them because of teasing. Such an explanation only gives attention to the undesirable behavior. Just observe and then make what changes are necessary and possible.

The second positive action is to pay attention to your 12-year-old for the good things she can do. Teasers are generally very active, energetic children. When motivated, they can become the hardest-working members ever to bless a family. Give her household jobs such as cooking, cleaning or outdoor work. If she does not know how to do these tasks, teach her. To develop her motivation you might pay her or let her work toward some large purchase which she desires. Emphasize what a good worker she is and how much you need her around the house.

When a difficult situation persists in a family, the usual reaction is to scold and criticize the children who are provoking each other. Scolding and criticism do not work. Changing the environment and building on the positive behavior of your daughter involves effort and trouble for you. But you *can* take steps to resolve the situation effectively. Even more important, you can help your children with one of the most important lessons of family life, learning to live harmoniously with other people.

# Close Sibling Rivalry

**I have two little girls, a fourth-grader and a fifth-grader. They don't get along well together, and their attitude is upsetting our whole family. They fight and argue almost constantly, and every time one has some good thing happen to her, the other one seems terribly jealous. Is there any hope for peace and harmony?**

One of the problems of having two children of the same sex close in age is the situation you describe so well. They seem to go through a period, particularly during the elementary school years, when they are truly the best of enemies.

One solution recommended in some childraising books is not to have children closer than three years apart. It is a little late for that solution in your case (and in ours), and we think it is a very poor solution anyway for reasons we shall explain.

The first step for you — and it is not an easy one — is to forget the negative factors in the relationship of your girls and to focus on the positive factors. There aren't any? Think harder.

First of all, your girls are learning about human relationships even as they do battle. It is a subject none of us ever masters, so let's not be too hard on nine- or 10-year-olds when they are less than perfect at getting along. Children without close siblings are sheltered from this experience it is true. But where are children better exposed to the good and bad of living with other people than in a warm, loving, supportive home which allows them the freedom to face and work out problems? So let's realize that our children learn from their battles just as they do from kindness given and received.

What other advantages do your girls share? Do they share the same room? Sleeping in the same room gives one a companion to face the scary shadows and the "things that go bump in the night." Are they close enough in size to share clothes? If so, they can double their wardrobes. And while a sister may not be a favorite companion, particularly at this age, one never lacks another person to play with.

Last of all, remember that sibling rivalry seems to peak and ebb. This bad time will pass. Were your girls companions in mischief when they were preschoolers? They may well grow into good friends again. This will be a considerable advantage when each needs a friend and confidant of the same age during the difficult adolescent years.

Think out these advantages carefully in your own mind, then focus on the advantages rather than the disadvantages in their relationship. It might be reflected only in casual remarks from you: "Janie, aren't you lucky to be able to wear Suzie's clothes!" Or "Sleep in your sister's bed when you are scared at night." Or, "You two are certainly getting good at that game. It must be because you play it together so often." The important thing is to maintain a positive attitude.

When the arguments and the jealousy peak, avoid critical remarks that draw attention to such behavior. The remarks simply don't work. Instead, try to anticipate the difficult times and separate the girls for those activities. Let them help you in the kitchen, but appoint one helper at a time. If you are going shopping, take one companion at a time. It might be more trouble for you, but the opportunity to enjoy the trip with one companion rather than enduring it with two more than makes up for the extra trouble.

If having friends over is an occasion for rivalry, again take turns. Allow one girl to have a friend over for dinner or overnight. Next time the other girl gets a turn. This way no one has to outdo the other.

We are convinced that having brothers and sisters is an advantage for children and that the good times in their relationships far outweigh the bad. Nevertheless, there are problem moments when parents must take that statement on faith alone. In such times, focus on good behavior, ignore the fighting and arguing, and adjust the environment so that these negative encounters are minimized.

# Allowances

**I am thinking about starting my oldest child, a first-grader, on an allowance. Could you give me some ideas about managing children's allowances?**

We think allowances for children are a good idea. We live in a society where most transactions involve money. Helping a child to learn money management is part of parenting.

Allowances should start by age seven or eight. Before this time an allowance is a token. The child knows money is good to have and may wish to imitate friends or older brothers and sisters, but he has little sense of money value or use. The child will be equally satisfied with a nickel or a quarter.

Around age eight the child begins to develop a sense of ownership—of acquiring, collecting and perhaps hoarding goods. Research on child development from the Gesell Institute says, "Eights are money-mad."

Rather than viewing such behavior as selfish and undesirable, parents should recognize that the child is in a new stage of growth. The child is trying to sort out the concepts of "mine" and "yours" and what ownership means. An allowance can help him acquire this understanding.

An allowance is not a salary. It is a sign of unconditional parental love. It is the child's weekly share in the family wealth. He is entitled to it just because he *is*—no matter how lazy he is, no matter how badly he behaves.

When a child, young or old, cannot get by on the allowance, she has the same option as the rest of us—to work. We think children should do some daily chores simply because they are part of the household. On the other hand, if they do a special job which you would pay an outsider to do, then it is appropriate to pay them. We put window-washing and hand-polishing furniture in this category. For such jobs they deserve a salary. This, however, is not an allowance.

Do not withhold the allowance as a punishment. If you do, you make the allowance a reward or "pay" for being good. In order to learn responsibility, the child must be able to count on the allowance.

The allowance can be used, however, to curtail waste. Suppose your child loses or wastes too much paper, paste, crayons, whatever, at school. You might make the allowance large enough to cover these items and have the child buy his own. Another plan, easier for eight- to 10-year-olds, would be to supply a reasonable amount of school supplies each month. When the child runs out before the next month's supply, he must supplement from the allowance.

An allowance is not an expense account. Let the child have as much choice as possible in spending the money. Don't pressure. Specify the weekly sum. If there are some necessities which must be purchased out of that sum, specify those too. But remember, without freedom of choice the child will learn little about budgeting and spending money.

If any purchases are forbidden, that too should be specified when the allowance begins. If you want to set limits on candy, soft drinks, war comics or toy guns, set them in advance.

The number of items which the child must finance and the amount of the allowance should both increase over the years. From third to eighth grade, we recommend a range from $.25 to $2.00 per week, increasing every year or two.

By high school a child can handle all his expenses except room, board and medical. Personally we can't imagine buying clothes for our teens. We simply wouldn't have the courage. For this we suggest an allowance of $25 to $50 per month.

The advantages of the allowance system are many. An allowance helps a child learn about ownership. It spares parents from the temptation to be arbitrary, rewarding children with money when life seems to flow smoothly and refusing their requests when things go badly. It frees parents from the hassle of making a decision over every trivial request: "May I have this?" May I have that?"

Through an allowance the child gains some independence from parents and some responsibility for meeting her own needs. It helps the child to grow.

## Money Education

**I have read your comment on children's allowances. I think allowances have some drawbacks. Children's needs vary a great deal from week to week. Isn't it better to see that they use money properly by giving them what they need each week?**

It is true that parents can control their child's spending better on a need basis. Adjusting for varying needs on an allowance system is no great problem, however. When you set an amount for allowance, plan to adjust that amount once or twice until you reach a sum both you and the child can live with. We support allowances because the education and responsibility which follow from the allowance system are important for the child's growth.

Money education, like sex education and death education, is quite neglected in our culture. It is almost a taboo subject. In fact, we know men who will talk about their sex life but will not tell you the amount of their salary or the extent of their indebtedness. Money is a sensitive area.

Small wonder that adults make such colossal blunders with money. They are suckers for impulsive buys. They get in debt over their heads. They are unable to be generous with their money. Why? Because they have never learned how to use money.

What is money? In the 20th century it is the very fruits of our labor. As such it is symbolic of our self-worth. When it is being distributed, money is power. If our children have money, they have power. Consequently, to give them money is to give them power—some measure of power over their environment.

That is the reason some parents are reluctant to give their children an allowance. If they do, they hedge the allocation with a number of shoulds and shouldn'ts.

When you decide on a case-by-case basis whether a child's request merits funding, you are exercising parental control, a good thing. But parents must teach children about money and prepare them for independence.

Each child from about age eight should be free to save his or her allowance, waste it, or give it away with no limitations. Each child must be free to make mistakes. The parent retains great control because the amount of money the child has is small. The child, however, needs an increasing amount with which to learn that, for example, if he buys candy, then he can't go to the movies.

As a child grows older, she can earn money for tasks at home and later progress to a job.

# Money-Madness at Eight

Our oldest boy is eight, and he has developed a new-found interest in money. We started an allowance and he was thrilled. At first his interest was cute, but now it is annoying. He wants to be paid for everything he does. He has plenty of spending money, and I'd like to change this attitude.

You have described nicely one aspect of the typical eight-year-old. Eights are growing up in lots of ways, and "money-madness," as Gesell describes it, is one aspect of growth. Your son's over-concern with money is normal and will probably disappear on its own.

Eight seems to be when children try to define for themselves what "mine" means. Of course, two-year-olds know what "mine" means, but for them "mine" means anything the child wants at the moment. Eights are struggling with a much more sophisticated concept. They recognize that money is important for older children and adults, and they want a share. Eights frequently become collectors, and their rooms bulge with matchbooks, baseball cards, etc.

Eight represents the dawn of a new level of competency. They can initiate and carry through more complicated tasks. Schools reflect this development in that the work in intermediate grades is quite different from the work in primary grades. Now children are capable of taking music lessons, joining teams, and participating in outside activities. While these activities will be appropriate for several years hence and, indeed, may be best postponed for a year or two, the ability to handle these interests begins around the age of eight.

Now is the time for you to build on these skills in responding to your child. He can probably handle more complicated jobs around the house, and initiate and follow through with little interference. This is not to say he will no longer forget jobs or postpone them (he might well!). But he is capable of jobs which formerly were too complicated for him to carry through alone. Some jobs he might handle: doing the dishes (as opposed to helping the parent as the younger child might), sewing buttons and hems, yard and garden work not involving machinery, and regularly assigned housecleaning jobs.

At times parents feel guilty about their child working. They feel they are depriving or abusing their child at an age when he should be carefree. If, however, you recognize the new skills your child is developing, you'll realize that assigning jobs is not abusive. It helps him develop his abilities and independence.

Whenever introducing a new job, it is important for you to teach carefully how it is to be done. You cannot assume a child knows in what order to wash dishes. Show him.

Next—and although this sounds contradictory, it isn't— once the child can do the job, let him do it his way, so long as it is adequate. No two homemakers run a kitchen alike, yet the tasks still get finished. Allow your child this same freedom. Don't nag or criticize him for doing something differently from your way. This hands-off attitude respects the fact that your child is becoming a competent person in his own right.

How do you know whether the assigned jobs are appropriate for his age and ability? Watch your child. If he is reasonably interested (few people are wildly enthusiastic about working) and does the job reasonably well, it's probably appropriate.

How do you handle his money-madness? Personally, we favor a no-strings-attached allowance and it is good to begin the allowance when his interest in money is high (See "Allowances," p. 59). Whether you choose to pay extra for certain jobs is, we think, up to you. If you feel he is doing more than an ordinary chore, and if you would pay a non-family member for the same job, we think it is reasonable to pay the child. The important thing is to spell out clearly *whether* he will be paid.

Avoid open-ended offers such as, "I'll pay you a quarter every time you clean the sink." In his zeal for money, he might do the job with greater frequency and enthusiasm than you anticipated. Then you are forced to change the job and he feels cheated.

Let his money obsession be. He will outgrow it. Instead, build on the new skills which are developing. The eight-year-old's money interest is not a greed sign but a growth sign: an effort to discover "What is mine?" in this world and perhaps even part of the effort to answer the greater question, "Who am I?" in this world.

# Music Lessons

**My eight-year-old would like to take piano lessons. Is this a good age to start? How can I keep him interested enough to practice?**

You are wise to recognize that practicing is the big bugaboo of the fledgling piano student. Some activities, such as learning crafts, may require no practice outside the lessons. Other activities, such as tumbling, require practice, but it can be done in the company of others.

Music lessons without practice, however, are a waste of time and money. Furthermore, the practice must be done alone. It is solitary, not sociable. Finally, practice must be regular. Although the beginner's practice session might be brief, it must be held every day. A long session once or twice a week will not work. Here is how you can help:

1) *Find a regular time for practice.* Many young children are worn out after a full day of school and are not able to tackle piano practice at 3:00 p.m. Early evening is a possibility, although the distraction from other family members and competition from homework and television pose problems. Early morning may be the best time for young children to practice. They are often early risers anyway, and they are rested and eager at this time. One full-time musician schedules all lessons for younger pupils before school. He finds they are freshest for lessons at 7:00 or 7:30 a.m.

2) *Help with practice.* You will probably need to stay with your young child for all or most of his practice sessions. If you know a little about music, it helps. Even if you do not, however, you can help him organize a difficult challenge.

Know what music has been assigned. See that he practices all his music. See that he goes over the difficult parts. Most children like to skip the hard parts and play what they already know well. Your task is to encourage him to practice the difficult parts. At the same time listen to the things he does well. The child gets pleasure and satisfaction from playing what he already knows. Help him balance the easy and the difficult.

3) *Provide incentives.* Enthusiasm for music might be enough to motivate your child. After a while, however, treats and rewards might also help to provide incentive. Food, money or a privilege might all be used as rewards. You might give a star for each practice. Four stars (four days) in a week merit a small treat; five stars, a medium treat; six stars, a big treat.

4) *Keep music fun.* If you start lessons, continue long enough to give them a good try. Expect occasional grumpy days. In general, however, music should be fun.

If your child develops a real dislike for practicing, stop lessons and introduce music in other ways. Select records which will expose him to music of all sorts at home. Consider the school band where most practicing can be done during school time. Or consider piano at a later age when the child is more mature and better able to structure his own time and practicing. The most important goal is not to make your child a great musician but to give him knowledge of and a liking for the great gift of music.

# Funerals for Pets

**My nine-year-old son's dog was killed by a car last week. He wanted to bury it in our back yard with a ceremony. I felt this would be sacrilegious since animals do not have immortal souls. My husband felt it would be good for our son and would not offend any Church teaching.**

We know of no Church teaching that says it is wrong to memorialize the death of a pet. Consequently, we see no reason why your son should not bury his loved pet with ceremony. Actually, it is probably a good idea to do so.

Death is a hard fact. It has been compared to a harvesting,

a transition, being called, a dreamless sleep, an ending. Death is many things. For those of us left behind, it is mostly viewed as the final and permanent departure. And that takes some getting used to. We need all the help we can get. We miss the departed.

Children naturally and correctly want to surround the hard fact of death with a liturgy. It is their way of handling it. The pet mouse or gerbil casketized in Mom's old jewelry box. The farewell song sung with friends over the grave of a pet bird. The wooden headstone carefully and thoughtfully carved for one's dog. The flowers planted on a cat's grave. A brief eulogy spoken to one's friends through the tears: "He was a good racoon." Children are learning to say good-bye.

Compare this with the horror our nine-year-son expressed when he heard we had simply flushed his dead goldfish down the toilet. "You didn't just put Goldie in the toilet? Not Goldie? That's no way to say good-bye!" He was right.

When we reach out to love another living being, even an animal, the relationship brings us joy and satisfaction. We enjoy the animal's antics, beauty and loyalty while it is alive. At the same time, by making the investment in loving an animal, we make ourselves vulnerable to sorrow when the pet is injured or dies. "I never want another dog," a child often sobs over his dead pet. As our children grow, we can help them to understand that even though loving a pet brings sorrow at death, we are still richer for the total experience.

"Good-bye, my friend. I shall miss you dearly. Your departure shall be surrounded with all the grace of ceremony that our attachment required." Ceremony is certainly good for those of us who mourn. Your son has good instincts in wanting to memoralize an important event.

# Regular Chores

**When is my child old enough for regular household jobs?**

The child who does not have chores at home at eight, nine or 10 has been sadly shortchanged. The child and the family all benefit from sharing chores.

Children who possess skills view themselves as capable. They have confidence in themselves, a sense of "I-can-do-it." Talking about your child's self-esteem is nice. Helping a child develop self-esteem through meaningful work is even better.

Children who do chores develop a more flexible attitude toward male and female roles. A house is not a place which mother takes care of. It is our family's dwelling which we all use, we all mess up, and we all put to rights again. Both boys and girls can do housework.

Children who do chores sense that they are needed. They are neither guests nor liabilities but valued, contributing members of the household.

The mother in a large household and the working mother have no problem about needing help. For various reasons mothers who have the time and energy to run a household alone are often unwilling to let their children help. Some mothers would rather do the jobs themselves than bother with a child's help. The message communicated is, "Children? Who needs them?"

Other efficient mothers let children do chores, then do them over again to meet their high standards of perfection. The message from this kind of mother is, "You are not capable. I am." The child's self-confidence is diminished by working rather than increased.

Sometimes deeper psychological reasons may account for a mother's unwillingness to share jobs. Accepting help makes her feel inadequate and threatens her perfect homemaker image.

Some other mothers may prefer to keep busy with housework so as not to face the challenge of filling free time. We recently talked with a middle-aged woman who, after many years of working outside the home, had quit her job. She confessed that she had cleaned everything in her house three times and was currently on the second cleaning of the garage. How sad that a person blessed with free time should be unable to find more constructive ways to fill it.

The woman with a home and family can anticipate the years when children and housekeeping will take less time and she will have hours free for other pursuits. We are not suggesting she abdicate her responsibilities in the home. We are suggesting she welcome the help her children can give and use the time gained for some other pursuit.

Perhaps the greatest favor a mother can do for her elementary-age children is to become involved enough in pursuits outside the home so that she *needs* their help. The children can discover that they are capable and important, and the mother can discover that there is more to life than housework.

Here are some tips on how to develop capable helpers among the elementary school set:

1) Select tasks within the child's capability. From around age eight onward, children can learn to do most housework, laundry and yard work.

2) Assign real jobs. Some mothers cook a five-course meal while Susie stirs the gravy. They then exclaim, "Susie cooked dinner." Such false enthusiasm is demeaning and fools no one, certainly not the child. Give Susie jobs which she can really do and compliment her for genuine competency.

3) Any chore worth doing takes time to learn. Most jobs for adults assume a three-month orientation period. Realize this and take the time to teach your child the right way. Many parents fall down on this point because teaching a task demands much of the parent.

Figure out step-by-step how you want the child to clean the bathroom. Write down each step. Most children like to follow a checklist and enjoy the satisfaction of reaching the end. If you do not specify each job, be assured it will not be done. (In our household, we realized that we had omitted "Wipe off the window sill" when, after three weeks, the window sill had not been touched.)

Work along with the child a couple of times. Demonstrate the task and give the child a chance to do it. Assign only the number of jobs you can teach and supervise.

4) Specify a time to do chores. If no time is set, the child can always promise to do them "later."

5) Do not expect your child to be enthusiastic about developing his capabilities and self-esteem through chores. Work is work. Most likely the child will gripe, and the object of his gripes will be you. As a good disciplinarian, you allow him to express his gripes, but you see that he does his chores.

6) Decide in advance whether the child gets paid, whether he gets some other reward, or whether he is expected to do this job as his contribution to the family. Children like to know where they stand.

7) Once your child can do the job adequately, let him alone when he works. Don't hover around, criticize or give advice. When he has finished, check his work. Point out any oversights, and above all, notice and appreciate a job well done.

Once again we stress that teaching children to help with chores around the house is not easy. In the beginning it takes far more time than doing it yourself. And you may find that the chore is not done exactly as you would have done it. When you find yourself lacking in patience think back to a time when you had to learn something. Were you always delighted at the prospect of new responsibility? And how long did it take you to learn what was required? Instant acceptance of a new responsibility and instant success with any learning task is rare.

# Gambling

**What do you think about children gambling? My husband and I were surprised while watching the Super Bowl on**

television to hear about our children's bets. Our 13-year-old had a total of $5 bet with four different boys. Our 10- and eight-year-old boys kept hoping Pittsburgh would not score again because that would put them over the point spread. Even our 12-year-old daughter, who doesn't know football from fox hunting, had money bet on the game. Should we worry about this? What should we do?

Children love to take risks and triumph against the odds. Even more attractive is the element of magic in gambling. Children are not so far removed from fairy tales. They have faith that dreams come true. Magically the dice will roll to the chosen number. They really believe they will win.

Seen in this context, the betting you describe is a normal part of growing up. Like most developmental aberrations, gambling requires acceptance and understanding on the part of parents, who perhaps can regard it with a certain amused tolerance.

"Gambling is an addiction," some people have claimed. That is incorrect. Gambling may be a very bad habit for certain adults, but it is not an addiction. Alcoholism, certain drugs, cigarettes, even some physical activities are addictive because they can cause the body to develop a physical hunger for the substance or activity. Although it may become a very bad habit, difficult to get rid of, gambling does not fall into the category of an addiction.

"Gambling is immoral," others have claimed. That too can be incorrect. In itself gambling seems to be morally neutral. It could be wrong if the gambler risks money that belongs to someone else or that is needed by the family.

Many adults enjoy playing bingo in church basements. They do not seem to be squandering the family bread money and they do seem to have a good time. Other adults like to play poker. Some of Jim's fondest childhood memories are being allowed to play penny-ante poker with his dad and uncles. They all took the game seriously, yet there was no

71

danger of losing one's bankroll. Nor did Jim grow up to be a habitual gambler.

Adults can now buy lottery tickets in many states for a weekly moment of excitement. Adults trade stocks and bonds, buy and sell gold, speculate on futures—all hoping to make a quick fortune the easy way.

At best, providing one has money to allot for this entertainment, gambling can be fun. At worst, gambling can be a very bad habit leading an adult to risk funds he has no right to lose. In the middle, gambling can be a harmless, morally neutral activity. In a growing child, gambling represents a normal stage of risk-taking and magical hopes.

So what should a parent do? We think you should do nothing. Many children try gambling, then grow out of activities such as you describe. Any attention you give, positive or negative, will only serve to make the gambling more interesting.

In a more positive vein, you might encourage your children in other activities that involve risk and magic. In competitive sports a child must set his skills against a peer and take a chance on his ability. Magic is more difficult to find in our real adult world. Card and table games, a magician's set, even the encouragement to read and think about fanciful adventure stories may help.

# Homework Battles

**Our 10-year-old puts off doing his homework. The more we get after him, the worse he dawdles. Can you help us?**

For some children arrival home from school is the signal for the "great homework battle" to begin. Often the child is already having some trouble in school and seems to need parental help. The "hostilities" may extend up to five hours in extreme cases. Father's temper, mother's exasperation and/or tears and the child's stubbornness all come into play. The child almost always wins.

Parents cannot force a child to learn. All the flash-card drill and rewritten spelling words in the world cannot substitute for your child's interest and motivation to learn. With all your drilling, lecturing and correcting, you may be strengthening non-learning by giving your child attention for it.

It is very common to nag dawdlers. So you end up paying far too much attention to behavior you would like to discourage. Although it is not easy to appreciate, even negative attention like nagging is sought after by the child. Instead of giving attention to dawdling, you need to focus on positive factors.

When you sense you are spending too much time on the dawdling, it is wise to get out. Leave learning alone. Try an indirect, more matter-of-fact approach.

It may be practical simply to set up a situation that is congenial to doing homework. When would your child like to do his homework? He chooses after dinner. Where? After ruling out the TV room, the dining room is chosen. You, your child and the teacher together decide that one-half hour is a reasonable duration.

You then see that the TV is turned low while your child is required to sit at the dining room table from 7:00 to 7:30 p.m. with his school books. You do not check on him. There are not even any subtle reminders like, "How's it going, son?" You do not go over his work or help him unless he asks you specifically to do so.

At 7:30 your child is done, whether he studied or not. You have done as much as you can do without reinforcing his non-learning.

In fact, you have done a lot. You have set a time and place aside for homework, both of which are under your control. You have avoided nagging. You have minimized distractions. The actual learning is up to your child.

# School 'Failures'

My 10-year-old son almost failed fourth grade. The teacher said he can do the work, but his mind seemed elsewhere. She said it was up to us whether he should pass or be retained. During his first three grades he got mostly B's. This past year it was D's and F's. My husband thinks we should keep him back. I feel we should get him special tutoring and keep him moving along. Please give us your ideas.

School problems are not rare. There are lots of explanations and many approaches depending on what you see as the major cause of the problem.

It is a wise first step to check for medical problems. Have there been any physical symptoms? Has your son been lethargic? Noticeably more nervous? A physical examination with your family physician would be a wise precaution.

Next I would check out his basic natural intellectual ability. How smart is he? How does he compare intellectually with his agemates? You already have his teacher's opinion. She told you she felt he could do the work. That suggests to us that he is of at least average intelligence; however, we would get additional opinions.

Ask the third grade teacher her opinion. If she is not available, ask the principal. You want to know if your son is of average intelligence or better. In technical terms you want to know if he ranks above the 15th percentile on IQ tests. An average IQ is 100, but anything above 90 would be within the average range.

If his ability is considered by teachers and shown by IQ tests to be below average, then his performance may reflect his actual ability. It would be a mistake to push him. Retain him, and let him learn along with his intellectual peers.

You may find, however, that his intelligence is average or above. Our next suggestion is to find out how much he has actually learned. A child can do poorly on homework and classwork but still be learning. Again, look to your teachers and school tests. Ask his teachers whether they think he has an adequate grasp of fourth grade material. Does he know as much about school subjects as the average fourth grader? Achievement test scores should indicate what level your child has attained.

Achievement tests are different from IQ tests. An IQ test measures innate intellectual ability. A child is compared to others of his age. An achievement test measures performance. A child is compared to others in his same grade. Although most of us achieve according to our ability, it is possible to over- or under-achieve.

If your son's IQ is average or above, but his achievement is below par, he may be suffering from a special learning disability. There is special help available through school psychologists for such problems. It is not likely, however, that such a problem would show up for the first time in fourth grade.

So let's suppose his intelligence and achievement are both within normal limits. You are, of course, worried that his achievement may fall below normal if the present situation continues. What can you do?

Sometimes school problems are correlated with other upsetting events. Most frequent are the loss of a parent, marital disharmony, the arrival of a new sibling, illness or injury to the child, or some specific trauma at school. If such an event can be pinpointed, then it may be appropriate to deal directly with the upsetting event. The school problem may take care of itself.

If no upsetting event is obvious, and intelligence and achievement are within normal limits, then we would agree with you about promoting him to fifth grade. A tutor may be a good idea to help matters along.

One final caution to you or your son's tutor. Spend at least as much time working on subjects where your son does well as you do with his deficits. It would be a mistake to drill endlessly on weak areas. He needs to know success. He needs to be reminded that he can do school work well. He needs the experience and joy of a job well done.

# Losing

**How can I help my child be a "graceful loser"?**

Every competitor—and every parent of a competitor—dreams of a moment of glory: the come-from-behind finish as the underdog beats the favored runner; the brilliant piano solo which wins first-place honors.

But in any given competition, most of the participants will be losers. One individual or one team wins. All the rest lose.

Children probably do not need help in handling victory. But parents are important in helping children learn how to lose.

When a competitor loses to a better performer in a good contest, he or she at least may have the satisfaction of a good try. More disappointing is the frustration that results when fate dashes long-cherished hopes: the swimmer who has been practicing all through high school develops an ear infection just before the biggest meet of his senior year; the voice student gets a throat infection on the eve of a major competition.

Such reversals are bitter blows. Life seems unfair. At these moments children need their parents.

In helping a child cope with disappointment, it is easier to give advice about what parents should *not* do.

1) *Do not deny the disappointment* with remarks such as "It's all right" or "It wasn't important anyway" or "Don't feel bad." The parents wish to spare the child disappointment. Denying the failure, however, is a lie. The event was important. The defeat is not all right. Parents cannot control

that part of the child's world.

2) *Do not criticize the opposition.* "Their team practices three times a day. No wonder they won." "That school recruits athletes. They don't even live within the school distict." Avoid sour grapes. Do not teach your child that he or she is so superior and perfect any loss must be due to the dishonesty of the opposition.

3) *Do not make excuses.* "You would have won easily if you weren't just coming off a bout with the flu." "The referees were terrible." Such remarks imply that losing is so unthinkable, it must be justified in some way.

What can parents do?

1) *Do be sympathetic and supportive.* Does your daughter feel so bad that she cries over the loss of a race? There is no shame in tears. You don't know what to say? Then don't say anything. Hug her.

2) *Do let the child express frustration and grief.* Sometimes the youngster is a poor sport. He blames the referees or makes other excuses for himself. At this time it is best to ignore the negative remarks. Good sportsmanship can be learned, but the moment of defeat is a poor time for a lecture or a formal lesson. Talking about poor sportsmanship only draws attention to it.

3) *Do compliment signs of "good losing."* Say something like, "I was proud of the way you played after missing that free throw." It is one thing to make an error. It is another to bounce right back. "I noticed you congratulated the winner. That's class.

4) *Once a child has expressed disappointment, do applaud all positive attitudes and new goals:*

Son: "We'll get 'em next year."

Dad: "You bet you will."

Winning is glorious. Losing can be bitter. But losing is also an opportunity to learn to cope with life. Children who learn to take a defeat with grace are growing toward maturity.

# Promoting Reading

**My 11-year-old son watches TV every spare minute. He never reads magazines or books. How can I get him to read more?**

That's a hard one, because watching TV is easier than reading. You can sit passively in front of a television set and still enjoy it. But if you sit passively in front of a book, nothing happens. You must work at reading to get something out of it.

Even so, there is much that is good on TV. Just because books have been around longer does not mean they are better in every instance. For example, a TV documentary or drama on slavery may well teach us more than a book or article on the same subject.

Following this notion, you may want to improve your son's TV viewing habits. Read over the television guide together at dinner. Pick out a worthwhile or fun program that the family might enjoy that night. Then watch TV with your son for a half hour or an hour. Set a good example in your own choice of programs.

Still, we understand your worry if TV has completely replaced reading. We'll suggest two approaches, one positive and one negative, to get your son to read more. You can try either one or both.

On the positive side, you might examine your own reading tastes. Select some books that both of you can read. Set aside some time for you and your son to discuss your mutual reading. Keep a check list of the books he has read so he can see his accomplishments.

The librarian at your school or public library should have many suggestions about reading material for 11-year-old boys. You might visit the library with your son for a late afternoon or evening session every two weeks. Dr. Nancy Larrick's *A Parent's Guide to Children's Reading* (Pocket Books, 1969) lists many books by age and interest.

Now for the negative approach: Limit TV. First, a caution. We would not come on authoritatively and prohibit TV viewing. That only makes TV a more desirable forbidden fruit. Apparently TV is attractive enough for your son already. Rather, we would limit the time he may spend in front of the set.

The average time Americans of all ages spend watching TV is slightly over three hours each day according to the 1974 Roper poll. That is up from around two hours in 1961. We think it is quite a lot of time. We can all get fat and lazy in front of our TV sets.

Suppose you tell your son he can watch TV for only two hours each day. He can decide when (before or after dinner) and which programs to watch. But you are going to limit the time. His program choice will have to be more thoughtful since he can no longer watch everything he wants. You will be a bit busier for awhile keeping an eye out to see that he does not go over the limit.

Your hope, of course, is that he will fill in the extra time with some reading. That's where the positive approach above will be important. So here's to more selective TV viewing and happy reading.

# Monitoring TV

**Are there any TV programs that you think should be forbidden to children? My children range from four to 11.**

We prefer to *encourage* certain activities and TV programs rather than to *forbid*. We would forbid a TV program only if we were sure harm would result from a child's viewing it. Otherwise, we prefer to limit hours spent watching and force our child to choose. If she chooses all crime shows, then we set out to distract her interest with some other worthwhile family activity.

We suspect your question refers to TV programs which feature violence and/or sex. Studies have shown that violence on TV leads to violent behavior only where the viewer is already predisposed to violence. For most of us, watching a violent TV show will not affect our behavior.

To apply this insight, if we had a child who had trouble controlling his aggressive behavior, we would limit his viewing of violence on TV. If our child were not unusually aggressive, then we would not worry too much about his watching crime programs. We would still probably try to involve him in another activity.

Much the same can be said for sex. There is the concern that watching a sexy show will lead a young child into premature sexual acts. The evidence does not support this assumption. In fact, the sexually explicit shows are probably less stimulating for children than some of the highly romanticized Doris-Day-type comedies. Children who are not sexually knowledgable are rarely stimulated by sexual themes. Actually they are probably bored. Forbidding such a program would run the risk of creating an interest where there was little or none.

There are some factors about TV which worry us more than sex and violence. Specifically, we worry about the subtle effects of passivity, belittling parents, and materialism.

Passivity is a life-style that comes from too much watching of anything and too little doing. The solution here is simple and two-pronged. Limit TV viewing hours to two or three per day. At the same time, provide other attractive family activities.

Many family situation comedies depict parents as clowns. Dagwood and Blondie are extreme examples. Frankly, we do enough stupid things on our own that we don't need any extra help. We can do without a steady diet portraying the parent as incompetent and ridiculous.

Most serious to us is the materialism and narcissism inherent in TV game shows like "Let's Make a Deal." I know a teen couple contemplating marriage who seriously plan to furnish their home by appearing on "Let's Make a Deal."

Of all the TV shows, these are the ones that seem to appeal to the seven- to 12-year-olds. Whether it is the gambling, the instant riches, or the emotionalism, our kids would spend hours watching game show after game show. What a false impression of life! Yet even here we distract and limit overall hours rather than forbid.

There is much that is good on TV. Spend the majority of your influence encouraging the watching of good TV programs and let the "bad" ones take care of themselves.

# Overnight Visits

**I have two children in elementary school, ages nine and seven. They are getting invitations to spend the night at friends' houses, and they want to invite friends here. I think they are rather young to do this. Do you think overnights for children are a good idea?**

In general we think overnights with friends are a good idea. We want to build a solid, strong family, one in which the ties will last. We also want our children to reach out from the family to others. In order to reach out, they must have the confidence that the world is a good place, other people are good and kind, and we all belong to one big family, the human family or God's family.

Now those are pretty lofty concepts. While we can start telling our children about them from an early age, essentially we cannot "teach" this idea. These concepts must be learned through experience and made one's own through personal conviction. An adult who expresses ideals about universal brotherhood and harbors great suspicion about the fellow next door has never made this principle a real part of life.

What has all this to do with children's overnights? Plenty.

We think overnights with friends are a concrete experience for children, giving them the chance to discover that the world is good and people are kind. They are a good way for children to reach out from the family.

At the same time we do not permit overnights indiscriminately. Since we have children in a wide age range, we have had not only the opportunity but the necessity of developing guidelines. Here are ours:

1) *Under age seven or eight,* overnights are granted cautiously and sparingly. Overnights with relatives are nice for preschoolers. If the relative lives in the same area and visits regularly, the overnight is almost sure to be a delightful experience. A visit of many days with grandparents far from home is apt to be too much change at this age.

We use caution in permitting overnights with friends. Children of this age often want overnights, particularly if older brothers and sisters have them. Many times a six-year-old seems so grown-up and self-assured that everyone, parents included, assumes the child is socially mature. But even precocious six-year-olds have been known to break down at 3 a.m. sobbing, "I want my Mommy!"

2) *Between age eight to 11* begins a real interest in overnights. Children are often so thrilled with the idea that they go overboard, attempting to arrange overnights every weekend. Sometimes they assume that with overnights go other privileges: staying up very late and eating many sweet treats. We wonder if these aren't the real motivation for the overnight rather than friendship. At this age we permit overnights but limit them to one or two a month. This includes both going to a friend's house and having a friend over.

3) *From 11 to 14,* roughly the years of middle school or junior high, overnights are quite important. These are the years when a best friend or a few good friends of the same sex are vital. There is much interest in and talking about the opposite sex, but the "best friend" or the "buddy" shares the deepest confidences. It is a time when children like to spend

overnights with these best friends, and we think they are particularly appropriate at this age. While we still establish limits, we are generous about them.

4) *During high school years* interest in overnights declines. High school students might request an occasional overnight when it is more convenient to stay with a friend, but they do not seek the experience and enjoy it the way middle-schoolers do. We always try to clear overnights directly with the host parents. That way we know for sure where our high-schoolers will be, and what curfews they will be expected to observe.

Thus overnights seem to go in a pattern—with the years of junior high school being the peak years. Within limits, they are a good and a fun activity.

# Junk Food

**I am concerned about the amount of junk food my children eat, particularly sweets. Although I try to serve only a reasonable amount of sweet things at home, they get sweets from friends and neighbors and buy sweets with allowances. How can I control junk food?**

You are right. Sweets are everywhere. Children get many sweets outside the home. Even schools and doctors' offices sometimes give out sweets as rewards. What's a parent to do?

You can try to enlist the cooperation of your friends and neighbors. Suggest treats you welcome for your children rather than criticizing the foods they have been offering. Since you cannot control the behavior of your neighbors, and since you probably do not wish to break up a friendship over this matter, the effectiveness of this approach is limited to suggestion.

Basically your control over sweets lies mainly within the home. Most eating is still done at home, and your efforts can make a real difference in your family's nutrition. As in other areas of behavior, you can try a negative approach, a positive approach, or a combination of the two.

The negative approach is to ban or limit sweets, trying at the same time to educate your children as to why sweets are undesirable. In our experience, this approach is valid but only moderately successful. Occasionally we have met a child so well schooled in nutrition, that he will refuse sweets remarking, "My mother won't let me have that. That's not good for me." We have met very few children like this, and certainly our own children would never make such a remark.

Limiting sweets can be done by a time limit or a money limit. For example, a child may spend 25 cents per week on sweets, or a child may buy sweets only on Saturday morning, the usual allowance day. Such practices can lead to long discussions ("Is a week up yet?" "Does sugar cereal count as a sweet?" "Can two of us go together and buy a can of pop?"). Such discussions are undesirable because they focus so much attention on buying-sweets behavior and because they wear out parents.

Another way of limiting sweets at home is to set a limit for yourself. Resolve to serve a sweet dessert only once per week. Such a limit helps you to kick the sweets habit and makes you feel virtuous rather than guilty when the cookie jar is empty. Another effective way to limit junk foods is simply to get them out of the house. Your children cannot eat what is not available.

The positive side of handling junk food is more challenging, more creative, and more fun. The important adage to follow is: *Eliminate the sweets but not the treats*. When we set about improving our family's eating habits, we often let a certain grimness creep in. We announce that we aren't going to have so many sweets in the future. Groans. We even make the absolutely wrong remark, that is, that we are going to eat only foods which are good for us. This is guaranteed to make children and even adults dislike the entire meal.

Treats belong with celebration and joy and feeling good to be alive. Eating together is meant to be a time of joy.

The good foods you can turn into treats include fruits, nuts, seeds, grains and dairy products. When shopping, consider buying a treat food from these categories. Nuts in the shell are a fun project for children. Peanuts are good but rather commonplace. Cashews, pistachio nuts and sunflower seeds are a bit more exotic. Popcorn is a nutritious grain which has the added advantage that children like to make it as well as eat it.

Dairy products can be used in many ways. Make exotic drinks using the blender. Try yogurt or cottage cheese dips for fresh vegetables. Buy new kinds of cheeses for the family to try. For a super treat, buy a fruit out of season— strawberries in January, watermelon in February—and serve it forth with the enthusiasm it deserves.

When fruits are in season, freeze your own fruits without sugar. Peaches, berries and applesauce freeze well with no sugar at all.

Serve desserts with a flair. Develop your own original combinations of fruits for dessert. Top each serving with a little coconut or a maraschino cherry. Invent suitable names for your desserts. Why serve fruit when you can offer "Mama's melon melange" or "Red, white, and blueberries"?

The advertising for junk food often emphasizes that these foods are treats. They belong with good times and celebrations, the ads imply. Try this same technique when you provide good treats for your family.

# Neighborhood Fights

Since my children were little, I have intervened in outside activities if I saw meanness or roughness. I have even sent children from our property if they were "fighting." Many children now do not speak to me, some parents are "cool,"

**and my children are not readily accepted. Is there a solution to this problem or should we move for everyone's sake?**

It sounds as though you have gotten yourself into a difficult situation. Yet there should always be room for a human solution if you are willing to be open. Moving is expensive.

There are several things you may want to think about before trying to reestablish friendships. First, let's make a distinction between gentleness and nonaggression. I applaud gentleness in both sexes. Children need to be taught to be tender, to love babies, animals, growing things, and even one another.

Yet children will be aggressive. They shout mean words. They fight. Some of this is natural and important for development. They are learning how to handle their aggressions. As they grow older, there should be less physical fighting and more arguing with words. But it would probably be a mistake to try to prevent fighting from the very start.

It is also a mistake to try to choose or forbid certain playmates for our children mostly because it is too hard to enforce. We all feel that certain youngsters have values quite contrary to our own. Nevertheless, it may be a good thing for our children to experience these other values while they are still under our influence. Once they begin school, we are no longer able to control their total environment. Better for them to face these other values now, while we can act as a counterforce. Let your children have their friends.

If you agree with our reasoning, your problem now is to get back into the social circle. For starters, share the problem with the neighbor you most trust. Ask her what to do. She knows the neighborhood and could give you some practical hints.

Then stop forbidding aggressive children from playing in your yard. Instead, see if you can't encourage a few rough-and-tumble games to channel some of that energy. An obstacle course set up in your yard is very popular with five- to nine-year-olds. You might even take the initiative and invite some of the youngsters over for a marshmallow or wiener roast. If this sounds like too much, perhaps having children come over one at a time would be better. Would your child like to invite a friend for dinner or for overnight?

You have two difficult problems. One is to rethink your feelings about protecting your children from the aggressive behavior of their playmates. The other is how to restore friendly relations in the neighborhood. It will take openness and humility on your part. We wish you well.

# Grandparents and Gifts

**My parents visit us frequently and they always bring the children presents. My children have come to expect presents, and they seem to look forward to visits from their grandparents purely for the presents. How can I handle the grandparents and how can I change my children's attitude?**

While you may feel your children are being selfish and greedy, we think they are only being honest. Adults have set up a situation in which presents go with visits. Under those circumstances, it is only natural for children to come to expect the presents.

If it is any consolation, you are facing a situation which has existed in all time periods and all cultures. Universally, grandparents can and do exercise their privilege of indulging their grandchildren. Grandparents and grandchildren can indulge each other, while the middle generation, the parents, must assume the role of the "heavy." Parents must set rules and discipline.

As parents we are often upset when grandparents indulge the children. If we analyze some of the reasons this behavior upsets us, we may be able to live with it more easily. The gift-giving might represent an attempt by grandparents to buy the affection of your children. It may seem that they are competing with you for the children's love.

The interaction may go one step further. By showing generosity to your children, grandparents are doing a kind thing for which you should be grateful. In other words, not only might you feel they are trying to buy your children's affection but, even worse, you are supposed to express gratitude to them for doing so. Because our own relationship with the grandparents is so intimate, seemingly small, innocent actions can upset us very much.

Basically, will the gift-giving harm your children? We doubt it. Will it turn their affection from you to the grandparents? Again this is doubtful. The gift-giving is probably more upsetting to you than harmful to the children.

We would simply thank the grandparents for the gifts without making it into a big issue. Let your children express their excitement over the gifts. Remember, if they greet grandparents with "What did you bring me?" it is not due to greed or a bad upbringing. The grandparents have asked for such treatment. So relax and do not scold your children or apologize. You might point out to your children that their grandparents are very generous, but they do not have to bring gifts all the time.

You would probably prefer that the children like their grandparents for themselves rather than for their gifts. If so, perhaps you can find ways for them to relate more personally to your children. For example, you might encourage the grandparents to take them out or teach them skills.

Grandparents have many skills to share. Knitting, sewing, painting, yoga or playing pinochle are just a few possibilities. Grandma might teach both boys and girls to cook. Making cookies or candy would be popular. Grandpa might share carpentry skills or teach the children how to fish.

Going places with grandparents is another treat for children, whether it is visiting another city, going to a ball game or going to a movie. Suggest the most appropriate activities, and see whether you can develop the grandparents' interest.

Try to relax about the gift-giving and concentrate on activities through which grandparents can indulge and treat your children in a most special and personal way—by spending time with them.

# Vocation Questions

**I am the mother of a truly marvelous 12-year-old boy who wants more than anything to become a priest. His IQ is above average, his personality is dazzling and his love for life is remarkable. If I had the power to manufacture a perfect child, I could not have succeeded as well. My only prayer is that I can guide him down life's road to reach his potential goals.**

**I have promised him I would gather information regarding his vocation questions: Can he go to a high school seminary? How can he best prepare for the priesthood? Can you help me with these questions?**

In a time of abortion and child abuse, it is nice to hear a mother speak out so positively about her son. It sounds as though he has quite a fan. You seem eager to support his decisions.

One word of caution. Be careful of encouraging him to come to a career decision too early. Twelve is still quite young. Most young adults of 18 are hazy about their life plans.

Most Catholic magazines carry advertisements for high school seminary/boarding schools. Large cities often have high school seminaries for day students. Your pastor can, of course, help you locate a high school seminary. You should have no trouble finding such a place.

High school seminaries, however, are becoming less popular. They have many disadvantages, the biggest one being that, unless you live in a large city, a boarding seminary would take your child away from home at the time he needs you most. Next to infancy, puberty is the most critical developmental period. Crises of identity, bodily changes, awakening sexuality, first job, learning to drive a car, and other similar events are best handled within a family.

Before making any choice of a lifetime career, we think we should encourage a breadth of experience in our children. Whether scientist, businessman or priest, a child should not zero in too early on a chosen profession. It is important to generalize first and specialize later. Some high school seminaries therefore permit a close relationship with other high schools and dating.

When you help your son choose a high school seminary, remember, he needs his family, he needs his adolescence, he needs a broad base from which to confront life whatever career he may choose. Finally, he needs your wise support in choosing his direction.

# 'Terrible Twelves'

You can always recognize a 12-year-old child. That's the one who is arguing.

The 12-year-old argues about anything and everything. But the main complaints fall into three categories:

1) *Parents are always wrong*. Their decisions about how late a child can stay out, where a child may go and with whom are particularly good targets to challenge. A statement is never taken at face value. Always the question is "Why?" or "Why not?"

2) *Parents are not fair*. The child's own parents fall short compared to others. They don't allow what other parents allow. Parents are unaware of this, so it needs to be pointed out frequently.

3) *Parents do not understand how much money it takes to*

*get along* and need to be reminded of this. They do not recognize how frequently another new pair of jeans is needed. They don't even realize the cost of a movie or a pizza.

Twelve-year-olds are taking the first steps toward independence. Almost all parents say that they want children to be independent. But children learn independence by practicing independence from someone, and that someone is precisely the parent and the family.

Independence is learned in small steps. Often the learning years, beginning at age 12, are stormy both for parent and child.

Here are some suggested ways to live successfully with 12-year-olds:

1) *Recognize that striving for independence is a step toward maturity*, a new capability in the child. This helps you take a more positive view of the 12-year-old's criticism and challenges.

2) *Anticipate arguments by setting some reasonable policies and sticking to them*. How often can the child go out at night? How late can he or she stay out? How often can she have friends overnight? How many pairs of shoes or jeans will you provide? It might take some adjustments to arrive at policies the parent and child can live with. At times parents might feel like constitutional lawyers drawing up "rights to live by." Nevertheless, the parent who can point to a policy already set down can minimize the number of arguments.

Despite forethought, arguments and criticisms will arise. It is impossible to set a policy that covers every situation in life. And 12-year-olds are experts at pointing out any inconsistencies in parental behavior.

3) *When arguments arise, try first to consider the complaint*. Perhaps the child has a reasonable request. If the child has band or athletic practice at a certain hour, he may request dinner for the same hour every night. That's reasonable.

4) *Parents need not always defend themselves*. When a

child criticizes, the parent's first impulse is to present his own side. The child, however, is not usually asking for an explanation. The 12-year-old wants to play "You're Not Fair" or perhaps "Getting Mother's Goat." When mother answers, she adds to the game. A noncommittal answer, "I'll have to think about that" or "You may be right," ends the game and the argument. Mother has refused to play along.

5) *Parents can encourage the positive aspects of independence.* A 12-year-old can clean a room or cook a meal alone and do it well. Often, both boys and girls can handle a paper route alone or do an excellent job of baby-sitting. Twelve-year-olds can help others with little direction from adults. They can shovel snow or cut grass for an elderly or handicapped neighbor. In short, they can work, help and serve in adult ways.

Parents can recognize and applaud the arrival of a new stage of growth. They can consider reasonable complaints and minimize useless arguments. They can encourage and applaud their children's growing capabilities to work and to serve. They might even discover 12-year-olds are nice people to have around.

## Twelve to Eighteen
# Teens

These are the years that most worry parents. They are the
trial years when all the big adult questions get trotted out
while the child is still at home. Often stormy, regularly
contradictory, the teen is struggling for an identity of his or
her own and the courage to face the world without the safe
harbor of the family. Problems like alcohol and pot, premarital
sex and abortion, truancy and running away may arise.
Parents want to know how to talk with their teens, what
guidelines to follow for dating and curfews, how to keep their
teens close to God and Church. Still more everyday are
problems of buying stylish (and expensive) clothes and stereos,
getting teens to go on family vacations and, in general, just
keeping teens a part of the family. The teen years call for
parental patience and skill.

# Communication

**I'm having trouble understanding my high school freshman son. He has gotten so quiet. I can't get through. I wish I knew what was going on inside his head. I worry that he thinks I don't care and that I'm not skillful enough or wise enough to communicate with him.**

You are right to realize that "understanding" is one of the most common definitions of love. Sometimes, however, we need simply to understand that the person we care about has a need to be quiet and reticent for a while. Teens and preteens have frequent periods when they retreat "inside their heads" and want to be left alone. That is part of growing up. Parents need to remain available, nevertheless, and make periodic efforts to draw them out.

Understanding does not happen by chance. Active listening is the best way to bring it about. Active listening means the constant attempt to echo and rephrase what the child has said until the child indicates that you understand. For example:

Jeff comes home quiet and unsmiling.

"Hi, Jeff."

No answer.

"Bad day?"

"Yeah."

"It gets you down when things don't go the way you want."

"Yeah. The teacher made us do our papers over. The track coach zapped me for being late. I feel like quitting."

"Everything went wrong, and you feel like quitting."

"Yeah. And another thing..."

Jeff becomes more animated. Because his dad gives no advice and makes no judgments, a quiet and angry boy is able to share his feelings, to put them in words. Jeff perceives his father as "understanding."

96

Feelings are important in communication. If parents are any good at listening, they will begin to hear the heart. Children should be allowed to express all their feelings, including the negative ones. Feelings like anger may not be pleasant, but it is far better to have them expressed in words than in behavior. Feelings arise in us unbidden. The child may be responsible for his actions, but not for feelings which he cannot help.

# Family Sharing

**We have three teenagers at home, and sometimes I feel they are just boarders. We don't seem to share any family life. We used to celebrate family liturgies, but they think this is juvenile. We are poles apart in our choice of music and TV. They are happy enough, I guess, but they are certainly distant. And they'll only be with us a few more years.**

During high school adolescents begin to go their own way. They are taking their first steps in drawing away from the family. This drawing away is good and necessary, a gradual weaning from the security of the home. We parents, however, wish they would talk to us and share their ideas and feelings— at least a little.

Parents may have to look carefully for areas to share with their teens. Sports is one possibility, either as spectators or participants. If parents are in shape and teens are enthused, they might play tennis or golf together—not all the time, but occasionally. Most water sports can be enjoyed by parents and teens together. Try watching track with a runner, basketball or football with a high school player. If you already know enough to enjoy the sport a little and ask an intelligent question or two, you are apt to find your child's commentary more interesting and enlightening than the TV announcer's.

While adolescent taste in television may seem totally removed from yours, look more closely. Besides sports you might enjoy some comedy shows, movies or specials together. Mention programs you are eager to see; you might have company. If there are shows that your teens watch faithfully, you can try them once or twice. If you don't like them, that's no crisis. Just don't criticize their taste.

If family liturgies seem too juvenile to them, you might get their suggestions. Preparing ahead may seem too much like an assignment. Brief, spontaneous prayer appropriate to the occasion may be the most attractive liturgy.

Family liturgy can be thought of even more broadly, however, than special prayers. Think of family liturgy as any event, ritual, or celebration special to your family. For example, what about dinner out with Dad, Mom and one teenager? This practice is particularly attractive in a large family. It allows for quiet conversation and a peaceful, leisurely, festive meal. Teens do love to eat.

Parents and teens can share family night once a week. If you make this seem like an opportunity for you to instruct your teenagers, they will resist. Instead, think of family night as a chance for family members to share ideas, entertainment, food, snapshots or old home movies. If family members take turns planning topics, there will be greater variety and more involvement.

At family night we have shared everything from a recording of Robert Frost reading his poetry to the Jefferson Starship, from wild card games to movies of "when you were little." The important thing in planning family night is for the planner to feel, "I'm sharing this [music, poem, idea] with you because it's important to me." Not everyone will enjoy every presentation equally, but in most cases everyone will listen and share because they appreciate the spirit in which the activity is offered.

Another very social opportunity for parents to share with teens is a family vacation. Once parents and teens get away from their customary friends and routine, there is a precious time when talking comes easier.

None of these settings or "techniques" get at the deeper questions which parents really want to ask: What are you going to do with your life? What do you want to get out of life? To give? What do you value? Do you value at all what we value? These questions are never asked directly nor answered easily. But parents and teens can share other interests and activities regularly. Then, when the moment is right, the deeper questions can be addressed.

# Family Vacations

**Now that our two oldest children are teens, they no longer want to come along on family vacations. Should we arrange to have them stay home or force them to come along in the hope we will have a good time once we're on the road?**

Parents are apt to be baffled about how to handle the question of family vacations unless they remember two important things about teens. First, the influence of friends is all-important. Therefore, while parents look forward to getting away from the daily routines, teens fear they will miss something. "If I leave," your daughter is thinking, "Susie will find another best friend while I'm gone."

Second, teens tend to distrust their parents' taste. Therefore, while parents look forward to new experiences and new locations, teens suspect that whatever parents plan will be boring. A worse fate cannot be imagined: to be stuck in your parent's company *and* to be bored.

Once parents recognize these facts about teen behavior, a family vacation is not only possible but potentially satisfying. The first step is to choose a vacation that offers something for everyone. What does your family like to do on vacation? Do you want to cover a lot of miles and see and do a lot in a short time, or do you want to relax, unwind and get away from the daily pressures? Getting away outdoors, whether camping or in a cabin, remains universally popular because fishing, water sports, hiking and campfires can be enjoyed by all ages.

Here are some questions teens often raise about vacations:

1) *"May I bring a friend?"* Once the vacation has been established, this is usually the next question. While it may be impossible in terms of space, this is not an unreasonable request. An only girl in a family of boys might enjoy the vacation much more if permitted to bring a friend. Having a companion might draw the teen away from the family but, on the other hand, both might be drawn into family activities. At any rate it should improve the vacation for the child involved.

2) *"How long will we be gone?"* If teens are reluctant, a maximum of one week is a good idea. The time can be sandwiched in between school and summer jobs. This allows time for the family to get away together and still not interfere seriously with individual plans.

3) *"Do I have to baby-sit the little one?"* When there is a wide age spread in the family, we find that teens enjoy their younger brothers and sisters for short periods, but they are dubious about 24-hour-a-day togetherness. On a camping vacation our teens appreciate having a car available and being able to investigate the nearest city on their own—not every night, just once or twice. On other nights the campfire is more appealing because they know they aren't forced to be there.

4) *"Do I have to go along?"* We do not like to force teens (or anyone else) to do things. But in this case, we *force*. If parents really include everyone in the choice of a vacation, keep it short enough not to interfere with other plans, and permit teens some freedom of movement, the teens are likely to enjoy it despite some initial grumbling. Vacation provides a unique situation for families to get reacquainted away from individual routines. This is an opportunity too good to miss.

# Guidelines for Dating

**I would like some practical advice about setting hours and regulating dating behavior for teenagers. I believe in giving increasing freedom as they get older, but what are some good guidelines at 13? 16? 18?**

A few years back Robert Paul Smith wrote a book entitled *"Where Did You Go?" "Out" "What Did You Do?" "Nothing."* Although written about younger children, that title sums up the conversation that frequently occurs between parent and teen.

Formal dating for many teens is practically nonexistent today. A group of boys or girls drive around in a car, looking for members of the opposite sex. They stop at a drive-in or a pizza place for food and conversation. They go "out," but they do not date formally. The old rule, "You may date at 16 but not before," is not relevant for today's teen.

Furthermore, the mobility a car brings means that it is virtually impossible for the parent to know where a teen is at night. Even a well-meaning teen cannot tell the parent where he will be. He is simply "out."

Despite this casual style of recreation, it is possible for parents to discover and apply guidelines. Here are three ways.

1) *Learn about community practices.* We are not advocating that parents go by the old teen argument, "Everybody's doing it." On the other hand, to ignore what other children in the community do is to overlook a valuable guideline. Other parents also wish to bring up their children well and safely. If other children are allowed to follow certain practices, you can probably let your child do so. If the seventh- and eighth-graders frequent a certain local movie house on Friday nights, if the junior high holds dances once a month, if high school dances last until midnight, it is probably all right for your child to participate in these activities.

101

2) *See for yourself what is going on.* If you are undecided about letting your sixth- or seventh-grader attend school dances, offer to chaperone. You will probably be warmly welcomed (the job is not much in demand), and you can unobtrusively learn what junior high social life is like.

3) *Use common sense to make rules that are clear and fair.* Since teens frequently do ride around or go from one place to another in the course of an evening, we find that regulating hours is more effective than trying to regulate where our child goes. We think that 10 p.m. is an appropriate deadline through eighth grade, 11 p.m. for freshmen and sophomores, and midnight for juniors and seniors in high school. We modify these hours for special occasions, but they are appropriate curfews for our community. The practices of your community may vary.

Once a child is graduated from high school, we no longer set hours. The child is an adult and expected to be responsible for his or her own hours.

# Extracurriculars

**Our oldest son is in high school. He is very active and likes to participate in sports and school activities. While I approve of these activities, they are scheduled so that he has little or no time for chores or family life. I believe mealtimes together are important, and I wonder whether we should support activities which separate the family so much.**

As a family who juggles schedules of children of all ages, we understand and sympathize with you. When your son is missing the family meals, the coach of his team is also missing his family meal. We doubt that coaches or players arrange these times by choice. Generally the inconvenience in scheduling results from the fact that many teams must share one gym, one track or one ball field. The crowded conditions mean that we are raising young participants instead of young spectators, and that is all to the good.

Despite the difficulties for the family, we would support your son in his activities. For any child, growing up means a gradual but steady growing away from the family. Children must move into many new areas and develop new competencies in order to become self-reliant adults. Sports and school activities are one of the principal ways young people can test out their skills.

Active children, however, need not quit the family during their teen years. Work out some compromises. If there are chores he must do, ask him to work out a schedule to fit chores in with his other activities. Perhaps he can be assigned chores that do not have to be done at a certain time.

Family time is important, but it need not occur at the regular evening meal. Find other times to be together. In good weather weekend picnics are a possibility. Saturday or Sunday night supper in which all family members share the cooking is another possibility. Some families find that Sunday brunch after Mass is the one meal in the week when all members can be together.

It is important that family members be together, but it is also important that they *enjoy* their time together. A "you-be-at-home-for-dinner-or-else" approach can lead to far more resentment and disharmony than unity.

The more family members you have and the more active they are, the more planning it takes to juggle individual commitments and family activities. Consider your task as a challenge rather than a chore. You will find that there *is* enough time for chores, family time and individual activities.

# Clothing Expenses

**Help! My teenage daughter is going to put us in the poorhouse. The problem is clothes. We have a moderate**

income, and I've always tried to keep food, clothing, vacations and all within our income. Now when we go shopping together the bills are all out of proportion to the rest of our expenses. She is only 14, and at this rate I don't know how we'll survive through high school. How can we afford a teenage daughter?

Anyone who has ever been to a shopping mall knows that clothing is big business and expensive. It's even worse for teenagers. From early on, teens are aware that the exclusive models from fashionable boutiques are more desirable than mass-produced, mail-ordered clothing. Teens are often still growing, and growth means frequent new wardrobes. Any style, as dictated by the peer group, changes frequently.

The easiest way for a family to survive teenage clothing, we've discovered, is to put the child in total charge of his or her expenses from the start of high school. The teenager's allowance should be substantial, but it covers (at least in our family) everything but room, board and medical expenses. (See "Allowances," p. 59.)

You determine how much the teen gets by estimating how much she needs and what you can afford. If you often shop with your daughter, you know how much clothes cost. In addition she will need personal and school expenses, entertainment, gifts, and perhaps other items you can determine together. We allow the same amount for boys and girls because we figure that boys need more for cars, entertainment and so forth while girls need more for clothes. You and your teen should understand the amount starts on a trial basis and may need adjustment as you try out the system.

You can pay allowance weekly, monthly, or several months at a time. A weekly allowance is easier to manage. An allowance at three-month intervals makes large purchases possible. (It's difficult to finance a new winter coat by the week.) We individualize the payment of allowances because we find that one child can handle three months' allowance nicely and another would (and did!) use it up within a few days. In some cases we even keep the balance sheet ourselves and dole out the monthly allowance as needed. Don't be critical if your child cannot manage money over a long period. Neither can many adults.

When you turn money management over to your children, you must make some changes in your attitude. You might want them to buy at least one dressy outfit whereas they are happy with blue jeans exclusively. Independence means you respect their decisions about clothes. You can no longer pick up that cute little sale item and charge your daughter for it. If she is typical, she won't agree with your taste, and she won't want it. You can mention that a certain store is having a sale, but let her purchase.

If you get hand-me-downs from relatives or friends, the saving accrues to your child, not to you. Often this produces a changed attitude toward hand-me-downs. A slightly-used winter jacket looks more attractive to a teenager when it saves his or her allowance rather than your cash.

The advantages of this system are many. First, your teenager handles responsibility and learns from it. Clothing is important, but it is not a life-and-death matter. A poor purchase is a disappointment, but it is a fairly harmless way to learn from one's mistakes.

Most important, letting your child manage money takes much of the hassle out of the parent-teen relationship. Teens know exactly how much to expect from parents. If this is not sufficient to meet their needs or desires, they know that a part-time job, and not pestering parents, is the next alternative. Your child might tell you wistfully that his buddy just asks and his mom gives him a dollar; deep down, however, he knows that asking for money is juvenile and managing money is adult.

Last but not least, your own budget benefits because you know, for better or worse, the exact cost of living with a teen.

# Sex Education

**Is there a book on sexuality and morals for teenagers? I would like to get one for my son.**

Sex can be approached in many ways. You ask for a book to give your son, and that implies you are viewing sex as an area where factual knowledge is needed. We agree that information is important. Facts about anatomy and physiology, knowledge about sexual behavior and technique, and antidotes for common sexual problems can all be put in a book.

You ask that the book cover morality, and we agree again that sex can be and often is viewed from a position of whether it is right or wrong. We presume you want a book that tells your son to avoid premarital sex and to be very careful of parked cars and touches below the neck. Perhaps such a book might even throw in a warning that if he should succumb irresponsibly to passion, he might get VD or initiate a pregnancy.

There are such books, but we are not going to recommend one. Much more important for you is to ask yourself what you wish to do for your son. What is meant by a "good" sex education? Is it a factual course, like plumbing, where the first step is to read a beginner's manual before dismantling the kitchen sink? Obviously, sex is much more than a collection of facts.

Is good sex education a morals course which consists primarily of cataloging all wrongs—actual, potential and possible? Unfortunately in the past many well-meaning families have taught that sex is not to be mentioned because it is so potentially wicked. When it is finally discussed, the first educative messages are moral imperatives to avoid certain behaviors.

We won't recommend a book because the most important *first* step in sex education by parents is to convey attitudes, not facts, not morality. While this should ideally be done before adolescence, it is never too late to begin.

1) *Tell your son that sex is important.* Sex is the way chosen by God and nature for human beings to exchange genetic information, to xerox themselves, to keep the human adventure alive in history. This activity merits awe and reverence, not double-meaning jokes and trivializing.

2) *Tell your son that sex is beautiful.* In sex not only are souls invited to begin an existence, but the lovers can delight in their union. What better way to express love than to pet and touch, to reach for intimacy in the struggle to become one in passion's embrace and its gentle aftermath. What better antidote to some of society's sick deviations than for parents to speak to the beauty of sex?

3) *Tell your son that sex is fun.* Why is this so hard for us to do? Are we afraid to admit this to our children? Who but parents should be privileged to convey the joy and pleasure of sex to children? That's what all the hullabaloo is about. Of course it is fun. It is meant to be.

Sexual facts and morality can come after the above groundwork has been laid. The attitude that sex is important, beautiful and fun cannot be learned from books but only from other humans—most appropriately the parents—who have developed this attitude within themselves.

# Bad Companions

I am the mother of eight children ranging in age from eight to 16. Our children go to school with all types of children. I have tried to teach them that each person is a child of God and should be respected. But how am I supposed to draw the line about associating with certain children whose background is immoral? One neighbor lives unwed with a man and her six children; two of these children (15 and 16) are pregnant and unmarried. And what about the child that proudly tells of smoking pot or taking drugs, or the one that proudly brags of premarital affairs?

Do I teach the way to live, try to give good example, and then leave it up to God to guide my teens in their companions?

"Avoid bad companions" is not nearly so clear and simple a directive as the old examination of conscience would indicate.

First, how do you judge a "bad companion"? Certainly we don't agree with the naive bigotry which proclaims Catholic kids are good; all others are bad. We also should recognize that people who look, dress, or talk differently from us are not bad. Adults often decide that people who lie, cheat, steal and abuse sex are "bad." Yet we know that terrible injustices can be committed by well-dressed business executives while enjoying their $20 (tax-deductible) lunches.

What is a bad companion? In general, when we have little concrete information, we would be inclined to give each person the benefit of the doubt. If our child likes this person, he or she must recognize something good and admirable which we perhaps have not noticed.

On the other hand, we personally draw the line at companions who brag about drugs and premarital sex. Preadolescents and young adolescents are highly susceptible to peer influences. If the companions are a couple of years older, as often happens, their actions can take on a glamorous or heroic cast. As far as we are concerned, that is an influence we do not wish to tolerate.

We do not attempt to play God and judge whether these people are bad. We simply decide that we do not want their influence on our children.

How do you deal with unwanted companions? The direct approach says, "You may never play with the Jones children." The Jones children, being off limits, become even more glamorous and interesting than before. Furthermore, if daughter ever wishes to irritate mother a bit, she can raise

108

the issue, "Why can't I play with Susie Jones?" Long fruitless discussions ensue.

An indirect approach usually works better. Encourage those companions you approve of. If one child persists in an attraction to the undesirable companion, try to make the association impossible: "It's too late to visit Susie" or "We're doing something else at that time."

Probably the most effective way to deal with children's companions is to encourage all your children to bring friends to your house. If possible set up a pool table or Ping-Pong table. Have board games such as Monopoly available. Make your home an attractive place to bring friends.

Hospitality naturally involves extra noise, extra food and extra confusion. Of course as parents of eight children, you are probably somewhat immune to noise. And popcorn and peanut butter sandwiches make acceptable—and cheap—snacks.

For a conscientious parent, the advantages of having teenagers at home far outweigh the inconveniences. You know where your children are and with whom. If certain companions are questionable, you can get to know them better. Even children you don't approve of can be made welcome within your home. When you control the atmosphere, it is doubtful they will exert so "bad" an influence.

Home is a safe place for your children to learn that there are all kinds of people in the world. Also, other people can share the wholesome loving atmosphere of your home. Perhaps most important of all, you teach by your own example that warm, loving hospitality is truly a Christian virtue.

# Back Talk

**We have a 16-year-old son who calls me names and tells me to shut up. When I talk about rules and going out at night, he tells me I don't know anything. He cares for his dad a**

little more than me because he gives out spending money for the weekend. Yet when his dad tells him to be nice to me, he just laughs. We also have three younger children. I used to be a happy person, but not anymore. What can we do besides pray?

Ouch! You have described beautifully a household in which parents have lost control. With four children to raise we can well understand that you want to make some changes. It will not be easy, since it is difficult to change a family interaction pattern.

What you have to do is take charge—and the sooner the better. Since you cannot change everything overnight, we suggest you pick specific areas of behavior—in your case, hours and back talk.

To set the hours for a teenager, you and your husband simply decide on reasonable hours and set them. *Period.* Generally it would be wise to consult with the child, but in this case you probably will have difficulty holding a discussion with your dictator.

Set reasonable hours according to the activities of teenagers in your area. When do dances, sporting events and movies end? When does the local pizza parlor close? You might set your son's curfew at 10 p.m. on school nights with one 11 p.m. and one midnight deadline per weekend.

When you tell him his hours, tell him at the same time what punishment he will receive for breaking curfew. Set a reasonable punishment which you can enforce. Do not drag out punishments for days or weeks on end.

Loss of privileges and doing extra jobs are effective punishments for teens. Loss of privileges might include staying home after supper, no use of the family car (if he drives), or no permission to attend a special event such as a rock concert. Penalty jobs might include washing woodwork, walls or windows or cleaning the basement or garage.

When you institute a new rule such as a curfew, you must

be home to enforce it personally. Since your son does not take you too seriously, expect him to break the curfew. Then be sure you enforce the penalty. The message you must convey is that you mean business.

To enforce other rules follow a similar procedure: Select specific behavior. Tell him exactly what you expect. Tell him the penalty for breaking the rule. Enforce the penalty if he breaks the rules. Do not make too many rules. Aim at one or two things that are important to you and enforce those rules.

Back talk is the most difficult of all to handle, in one sense, because you cannot define the behavior specifically. "Be home at 11 p.m." means only one thing. "Don't talk back" can mean many things and leads to endless discussion.

"I wasn't talking back!"

"Yes, you were."

"No, I wasn't."

To avoid such useless discussion you can do one of two things. You can define the language you will not accept ("You may not tell me to shut up, and you may not charge that I don't know anything.") The other alternative, and the one which we prefer, is to ignore the back talk.

"You must be in tonight at 11 p.m."

"Shut up. You don't know anything. I'll be in when I feel like it."

"I'm sorry you feel that way, but your deadline tonight is 11 p.m. If you're late, you'll have to clean the basement before you go out again."

With this approach, you do not have to insist on respect. You will *earn* respect by the way you handle your son. We think the back talk will automatically lessen.

The practice of doling out spending money each weekend has drawbacks. It seems to buy your son's affection and it does nothing to teach him responsibility in handling money. A regular allowance is a much better plan. (See page 59.)

Finally, never focus solely on the bad behavior of your child. Even as you get control of his behavior, notice the things he does well. Make a list to remind yourself. Maybe he is a good student, athlete, musician, friend, big brother, worker, driver. Whatever things he does well, pay attention to them.

You want your son to live within reasonable rules, but you do not want to destroy your relationship with him or his spirit. You can both enforce rules and appreciate him as a person at the same time.

Regaining control of your children will not be easy at first. By all means pray. Pray for patience, courage and strength to do your job. Do not pray for some miraculous change in your son's character. That is asking God to do your job for you. Instead, pray with confidence that God will give you the grace and strength you need to fill that most challenging of roles: parent.

# Bad Language

**What can we do about smart-mouthed teenagers? We have three teenage children and their language is getting to me. They always seem to be putting each other down, and every other expression is crude and vulgar. Sometimes they use the same language on us. If I comment about their language, they tell me everyone talks that way.**

Welcome to the club! Not to be facetious, but many parents of teenagers are experiencing just what you describe. Modern teens use language we never would have thought of using and, as with other things, girls too are involved.

As with other areas of discipline, you are faced with the paradox that paying attention, even by criticism, can serve to encourage rather than discourage the behavior. On the other hand, as parents you are still in charge of your household. It is your prerogative to determine what kind of language you will tolerate in your home. We think you can lay down the law to your teens fairly directly and realistically. Tell them specifically what words or classes of words you will not tolerate.

Do not make a general prescription such as, "I won't tolerate disrespect." Such an edict can lead to endless discussion about what constitutes disrespect. Then you are paying far too much attention to the behavior you wish to minimize. It can be difficult to distinguish back talk from legitimate disagreement. On the other hand you can say that blasphemies, obscenities and/or bathroom talk is out. This is specific and direct.

There are a couple of pitfalls to avoid when dealing with smart-mouthed teens. First, their language can make you angry quickly and you will find yourself answering in kind: sarcasm in response to their sarcasm; put-down in response to their put-down. Communication quickly degenerates under such circumstances. Don't let it happen. Count to 10. Bite your tongue. Keep cool. Don't respond to an adolescent by acting like an adolescent yourself.

Another common response when emotion runs high is to make threats. "If you talk like that, you'll never again...," says Dad. When parents make threats, their statements lose their effectiveness. Both teens and parents know that drastic threats will not be enforced. So keep calm and don't threaten.

The kind of language you will tolerate in your house is up to you. Some households allow little back talk at any age. In other households people of all ages speak out rather freely and some sassiness is tolerated.

There are many factors to consider. Unkind words between family members may contribute to a tense, unloving family atmosphere. Younger children may pick up and imitate adolescent smart-mouths. On the other hand, forbidding all negative expression may result in a complete breakdown of communication between parents and teens. Soon the teenagers share nothing with the rest of the family. You must weigh the alternatives and choose the style with which you feel comfortable.

Whatever you decide about language, remember that it is *behavior* which is your first concern as parent and disciplinarian. In our house, for example, we are rather tolerant of language. We discipline behavior and never mind the mouth.

Are they *doing* what they were told? Curfew is at 11 o'clock. Our teens may have choice words about the unreasonableness of their narrow-minded parents. That we'll tolerate. But they had better be in at 11 o'clock. It is the behavior we insist on.

We treat blasphemy and obscenity as vulgar and in poor taste rather than sinful. We respond to such talk in the same tone of voice that we use to advise, "Don't pick your nose in public." No big issue is made of it, yet it is not considered acceptable.

Your style may be different from ours. Whatever language you decide to tolerate, tell your teens directly. Enforce what you say without reverting to their language or style. And regardless of the language they use, insist that your teens observe the rules of the house.

# Spanking

**My husband and I disagree about the discipline of our children, particularly the oldest, a 13-year-old girl. He spanks her when she does something wrong. I think she is too old for this. What do you think?**

We agree with you that spanking is inappropriate for 13-year-old girls. Spanking is demeaning. Spanking treats your daughter as a young child at the very time she is beginning to realize she is growing up. Other means of discipline are more effective for adolescents.

The most effective punishments for older children and adolescents are extra work and loss of privileges. Depending on the offense, a 13-year-old can be assigned to washing windows, washing woodwork, cleaning the basement or garage, or similar tasks. Such jobs are real and necessary work. They are within the capability of the child, and they are fairly unpleasant for most people, which puts them in the category of punishment. Loss of privileges can mean no movie on the weekend or no overnight at a friend's house.

Thirteen, the beginning of the teens, marks a new period in the discipline of a child. That wise father and fine writer, Eugene Geissler, notes that Christ went off from his parents at the age of 12. He suggests that around this age all children must begin to move away from the home, to do things on their own, to take the first steps toward independence and adulthood. As parents we must make the delicate judgment of when to restrain and when to let go.

If your daughter needs discipline all the time, perhaps you are still treating her with the restraint needed for a young child. Perhaps you need to allow her more room to do things on her own and to make her own decisions. Look around for friends who have teenagers and who seem to discipline them in a way which you admire. Talk to them frankly about handling a 13-year-old. They will probably be flattered that you admire their judgment and eager to share their views.

Make rules that are clear and fair. Be specific about such matters as where she may go and how late she may stay out on school nights, on non-school nights. What time is bedtime? What jobs is she responsible for? What are the consequences of breaking these rules? Clear expectations let your daughter know where she stands.

Support your daughter. Thirteen is an age of tremendous uncertainty. A girl often feels she has no friends, she is not popular, no one likes her—even though there is no evidence to support her fears. Emphasize the things she does well. Sympathize when she hurts, but don't tell her she is wrong or silly. For her the problems are real.

Finally, allow room for moodiness, outbursts and back talk. Thirteen can be an explosive, up-and-down age. If you forbid all expressions of feeling, you are apt to develop a teenager who stays in her room and never communicates anything to you.

Be clear and firm about what she must *do,* but be tolerant of what she *says.* Admire what she does well whether in school, sports, hobbies or at home. Be flexible enough to realize that disciplining a teenager requires growth on your part as well as hers. And when you must punish, use adult tasks rather than direct physical control which demeans.

# Running Away

**Last week after my husband and I had an explosive session with our teenage daughter, she ran away from home. She literally packed a suitcase and took off. She was gone the entire night. We found her the next day staying at a friend's apartment and trying to find a ride out of town. I'm angry about this, yet I'm afraid she will do it again, so I don't know how to handle it. She is home now, for the moment anyway.**

If you are like most parents, your runaway child has severely jolted your confidence in yourselves as parents. When a child runs away, the parent is apt to feel angry with the child. At the same time one feels like a total failure as a parent. Before you can deal with your daughter, you must deal with your own feelings about yourself as a parent.

The fact that your daughter ran away need not indicate you are a failure as a parent. Other factors are at work here which you might reflect upon.

First, running away among teenage girls is on the increase. Since women have so many opportunities today and, at the same time, such confusion about the role of women, the teenage girl is in a particularly stressful situation. While she does not know just what being a woman entails, your daughter does know she can try daring, independent actions formerly reserved for boys—such as running away.

Second, not all pressures on teens come from home. Teens are beset with all kinds of pressures from school, peers, perhaps a job. When enough pressures build up they, like adults, sometimes just want to escape from a too painful situation. While a fight at home may have triggered the behavior, there are other factors in your daughter's life besides her home.

Third, as strange as it sounds, running away indicates some positive things about your daughter. A teenager must be a rather strong and independent person even to try running away. While strength and independence hardly seem like virtues when used against parents, they are actually necessary qualities for teens to develop if they are to cope with the world on their own within a year or two. Somehow you are raising a strong, independent daughter, and that part is all to the good.

What you want to find out in dealing with your daughter is: Why did she run away? What is so difficult about life at home? How can life at home be made more pleasant for you and for her?

Frequently after a crisis both parents and teen can be more open with their feelings about certain situations. This means you must express your own feeling about the incident. Telling your daughter she has been bad and must be punished tells her nothing about how you feel. It would probably lead to angry silence on her part. On the other hand, telling her how concerned you were when she was gone, how relieved you were to find her, and how much you want to make home a happier place for all concerned is telling how you feel. Given this message, your daughter may tell you how she feels.

In regard to discipline, the parent of the runaway is tempted toward one of two extremes: either to be so severe she will never try that again or to be very lenient for fear she will run away again. Actually there is no way, either by force or by emotional pressure, that you can prevent your daughter from running away. If she wants to, it is easy. That is why it is so important to find out how she feels and what she wants and expects from her home life.

A behavior contract might help you through this stormy time in parent-teen relationships. What behavior of hers is important to you: regular attendance at school? achieving certain grades? getting home on time? doing household chores? What rights or privileges does she want: later hours? permission to go places? use of the car?

In a behavior contract you spell out the demands that are important to you; she spells out the privileges that are important to her. By mutual agreement, when she meets your demands according to the contract, she gets the privilege she desires, also as spelled out in the contract.

The behavior contract helps parents and teens deal with an issue in a fairly factual manner at a time when emotion runs high on both sides. It helps both sides express what they really expect of each other. It helps you to discipline in a reasonable manner at a time when it is easy to become too lenient or too severe.

# Broken Trust

**Our 14-year-old daughter told us she was baby-sitting for a friend the other night. By accident we found out she went to a party instead where drinking and drugs were present. When we confronted her with her lie, she answered, "If I told you the truth, you wouldn't have let me go." She's right. Now my husband and I are totally dismayed. We have**

lost faith in our daughter's word. In fact, I'm feeling very hateful toward her. Things can never be the same between us. What are we to do?

You have obviously been hurt. The first time a loved one lies to us feels like a betrayal. Once trust has been violated, you begin to doubt everything. We once overheard a conversation that went like this: "Are you telling me the truth?" "Yes." "Swear to God?" "Yes." "Why are you lying to me?"

The only solution is to quit asking for the truth. Avoid long debates about whether your daughter is lying. Such debates give too much attention to behavior you would like to eliminate.

Instead, retreat to a consideration of behavior that you can directly observe. Probably the simplest approach would be to insist on a curfew. For example, you might require your daughter to be home for dinner and home by 9:00 p.m. at night. You could extend that to 10:00 p.m. on nights with no school the next day.

Concentrate on getting her home. This means she cannot baby-sit after 9:00 or 10:00 p.m. No exceptions. There is no longer any profit to lying.

Your daughter will feel she is being imprisoned. She never gets an occasional late night anymore. Not for baby-sitting. Not for a party. Not for anything. Here is where you might negotiate a "behavior contract" with her.

These issues are brought to the bargaining table: She wants to stay out later sometimes. You want her to come home on time. Suppose you agree that every night she gets in before her deadline, she earns a bonus point. Each bonus point is worth an extra half-hour out. In other words, you agree that, if your daughter gets home most of the time before her deadline, she can earn occasional late nights.

Both of you gain. Both of you give up something. You would be giving up the right to say each time whether she can stay out later or not. If she has the points, she can. If she doesn't, she cannot. You would be agreeing not to decide on the merits of each case.

You would also be giving up the attempt to quiz her about where she is going or where she has been. As long as she gets home on time, she has the freedom to go where she wishes.

Curfews can be altered to fit the case. The hours given here are only an example. If you think they give your daughter too much freedom, shorten the hours. But remember, you have to give some freedom. She must have some incentive to keep her part of the contract.

Also, she is growing up. She needs to be free to choose her companions and activities to some extent—to the extent determined by the time limits you set.

You said things would never be the same between you and your daughter. Never say *never*. A behavior contract may give you some breathing space. It can get you out of a situation where you are constantly worried about truth and falsehood and where emotion runs high. It can make it possible for trust and love to return in time.

# Lying

**We would appreciate some advice on dealing with truthfulness from our children—a trait we have always emphasized as absolutely necessary for sound character. On several occasions our 17-year-old has told outright lies to us and, aside from confronting our child, we are at a loss.**

Lying in teens is rather different from lying behavior in younger children. In earlier years, lying may be partly motivated by fantasy or by a need to obtain attention. As a result, it can often be more directly dealt with. In teens, however, lying is primarily motivated by self-interest. Consequently with teens the best strategy is to make lying both useless and unnecessary.

Stop asking questions that invite untruthful answers. After all, our legal system never obliges a defendant to incriminate himself. Too often parents expect that very thing. Then they are dismayed when their child alters the truth for self-protection.

"Have you been drinking?" "Where have you been?" "Have you been out with Bill again after we forbade you to see him?" In response to the above questions, the teen may perceive that it is in his best interests to lie. He will clearly pay some penalty for telling the truth. Parents might resolve the problem by according their children the same right our legal system accords all of us. No one has to tell on himself.

We can hear readers saying that we are being too permissive. No, we are just being practical. If you are getting lies now, why set up further opportunities for lying? Even worse, why force issues to the point where not only trust is gone, but perhaps the child as well?

Instead, why not retreat to situations where you can believe your child? Parents should expect behavior from their teens that they can verify, either by their own observations or by the report of other adults. If your child is obviously drunk, or if you clearly smell alcohol on his breath, and this is against your rules, then confront him. Tell him, don't ask him. If you are worried about bad places or companions, then set a curfew. Check on the curfew, not the companions. To ask whether he has been at a certain place or with certain persons invites lying because you cannot verify his answer.

We are not suggesting that parents accept any and all behavior from their teens. On the contrary, we urge you to supervise your teens effectively by setting and insisting on house rules which you can enforce. Rely on your own personal observation to check on your teen rather than posing questions which invite lies. Grant your child that respect and you will find it easier to maintain or restore trust.

# 'Living Together'

**How do you deal with a 17-year-old daughter who plans to live with her boyfriend? She has one friend who is already doing this. She will be graduated from high school this summer, and she plans to move in with him after graduation.**

Living-in arrangements are a problem parents seldom had to deal with in previous times. Nowadays, however, many older teens are beginning to regard living-in quite casually. The influence of the peer group (her friend is doing it), the new morality (everybody's doing it, she thinks), women's lib, some elements of defiance (won't this be a shocker, she hopes), and the fact that she likes the guy—all are elements which might influence her behavior.

You, on the other hand, do not regard living together as casual. You regard it as a serious step of which you disapprove. This is not the same as being an hour late after a date. *Tell her.* You are entitled to make your opinion known.

Tell her why you disapprove. If your main reason is that Grandma will be shocked, she probably will not be impressed. If you believe that sex goes with commitment, and that commitment is established in marriage, you are apt to be talking language she understands.

In talking to her, try not to tell her about what is wrong with her. Remember, she is the expert regarding herself. Instead, give "I-messages." Tell her how *you* feel and why. You are the expert in regard to your opinions and feelings, and you are entitled to express them.

You can also tell her that you will not permit her to do this.

Suppose that she simply defies you. She does go to live with her boyfriend this summer. It is important to communicate that you do not reject her as a person. While you may regard this behavior as very serious, she may regard it casually. She may be back in a few weeks or months. To forbid her ever to enter the house, to disown her, to cut her out of your will, to refuse to speak to her on the phone—any such actions draw lines of battle which could separate her from the family forever. Make it clear that she is always a part of the family if she chooses to be.

On the other hand, since you do see her behavior as a serious violation of your principles, you certainly would be contradicting yourself to support her financially. If she is an adult, capable of supporting herself and arranging her own life, she is free to make her own decisions. You must recognize this. At the same time, if she is an adult, she is responsible for herself and does not depend on you for loans, meals or laundry services.

As a parent you are apt to feel that you have failed in some way. It is important for you to recognize that there are many, many influences which affect young people today. If we parents were to dwell on failure every time a child acted against our wishes, we would rarely make it past the toddler age. Besides, dwelling on failure is counterproductive. It doesn't get us anywhere. Instead of focusing on your success or failure as a parent, accept this situation as yet another challenge. Try to assess the problem fairly, neither minimizing nor maximizing her behavior.

The real failure in this situation would be to cut your daughter off from her family forever. Communicate that you love her but, at the same time, that you cannot approve of what she is doing. Be firm about not supporting her financially or in spirit, but realize that she is capable of making her own decisions. To avoid cutting her off, always keep the lines of communication open.

Whether she returns to the family again or only comes back to visit, welcome her into your home. If you have been frank and open about your feelings, she knows your position. Reminding her of her "bad behavior" will only sour the relationship you are trying to keep alive.

# Pregnancy

**Our 16-year-old daughter is two months pregnant. We just found out and we don't know what to do next. We want to help her as best we can. She has ruled out abortion.**

You have brought up a situation which has occurred in many families, including ours. Many parents' and daughters' reaction is panic. Everything must be decided immediately. This is not true. Babies take months.

We reject the two traditional "solutions":

1) A daughter disappears for six to eight months ("She's visiting Aunt Minnie"), then mysteriously reappears and resumes her life. This approach fools no one and deprives the girl of familiar faces and surroundings during one of the most difficult times in her life.

2) The shotgun wedding. Some few teenage marriages work out beautifully. Most do not. A pregnancy is a problem, but a marriage at 16 and a divorce by 19 is a tragedy.

Two serious questions must be decided: how to handle the pregnancy and what to do about the baby.

The simplest way to handle pregnancy is for your daughter to continue life as usual, that is, live at home and go to school. It may not be easy to do this when pregnant; however, it may be the best alternative.

There is probably not a high school today that does not deal with the question every year. Few high schools would ban a pregnant girl from studies. The high school probably does not even have a legal right to do so. As for the students, they know where babies come from. They are not shocked.

A teenage girl who stays in her school can be a support to other girls who become pregnant. One young lady, when her pregnancy became obvious, pinned a button on her purse which said, "Give life a chance."

The girl who stays at home has her family's support, loses little time in school and has medical treatment in familiar surroundings. With a supportive family, this choice can be excellent.

If she is uncomfortable with the decision to stay home, check with your local Catholic family service or other social agency to find out what arrangements are available for her in another community. When a pregnant girl comes to our community, she can live in a family with small children and assist the mother in child care. She can get instruction for labor and delivery through childbirth classes, and frequently the childbirth instructor will assist her through labor and delivery. If such is your daughter's choice, look for a setting where she will have warm, supportive people to talk with as well as instruction for childbirth.

What about the baby? Should she keep it or give it up for adoption? This serious decision need not be made overnight. It takes nine months to get used to the idea of becoming a mother under average circumstances. Certainly the unwed mother needs time to think clearly. She will make better decisions when she has family support and is not panicked.

Encourage her to talk about her feelings. Do not force her into a decision, and do not take her every statement as a final decision.

If she leans toward keeping the baby, talk out the question: Whose baby is it? Grandma's or daughter's? Misunderstandings could lead to rivalry and jealousy between you and your daughter and confusion for the child.

Avoid telling her, "Don't worry about anything. We'll take care of all that later." However much you want to protect your little girl, she is facing an adult problem and must deal with it as an adult. It is not kind to gloss over the coming reality. What will she do after the baby arrives? Continue school? Full- or part-time? If you wish to help her, wonderful. But the child is not a toy for her to take for walks on weekends and turn over to Grandma other times. She should be responsible for her child's care or for arranging its care at all times.

What about finances? If you want to help, fine. This issue also should be spelled out in advance realizing that she is responsible for her child, financially as well as otherwise.

What about adoption? Talk about this option well beforehand. Your daughter knows or can meet people who have had good experiences with adoption. Talk with a social agency caseworker well in advance. She can help your daughter talk out her feelings and give her necessary technical information.

Again, your daughter should not be pressured. She can make up her mind after the child is born. Many social agencies involve the mother in the adoption and respect her preferences not only as to religion but as to age, family size, and life-style of the family which will get her child.

Should she see her child after birth? Emphatically yes if she so desires. A young woman who has faced reality throughout her pregnancy should not be denied reality at this point. She deserves to see for herself that her baby is healthy and beautiful.

Today, when abortion is an easy way out of a problem, an unwed mother is a courageous woman who needs and deserves our love and support. When she has a child, her gift is life. When she chooses to give her baby up for adoption, she gives life, then gives it away. Let us be as loving and generous with her as she is with her child.

# Interracial Dating

My daughter is away at college, 19 years old, and dating a black guy. I'm against this and she knows it. I've taught her not to be prejudiced and I'm not. But when it might come to intermarriage, I draw the line. Should I feel this way? She says she loves him but won't marry him for the family would disown her. I feel I have failed somewhere along the line. Could it be she is rebelling? I don't want her to make a

**mistake she'll regret the rest of her life.**

The question of interracial families is personally close to us. Our family includes biracial children. We number three races and six ethnic backgrounds within the clan.

The first point, and we believe the most important one, is that your daughter is doing nothing wrong. In our society black-white dating is almost unknown in some areas, but in other areas it is fairly common. It is unconventional, but it is in no way wrong. Since we are raised within a family and neighborhood, it is easy to fall into the notion that whatever family and friends approve is right; whatever family and friends disapprove is wrong. When we go against family and friends (or when our relatives embarrass us by going against them), we feel guilty as though we have done something morally wrong.

What family and friends accept as right is *convention*. Convention is not morality. Many times convention supports us in moral behavior. This is true when we belong to a vital and living Christian community. In Christian community members give each other example, encouragement and moral support in their efforts to lead more Christ-like lives.

In some situations, however, the conventional viewpoint is itself immoral. In cases where a property owner refuses to sell to a black or a Jew for fear of "what the neighbors will say," the convention of the neighborhood is based on prejudice. The reason your daughter's black boyfriend is not welcome in your home or neighborhood is prejudice. The fact that most neighborhoods, towns and cities in our country react this way does not justify the behavior. It merely demonstrates that the conventional attitude in most neighborhoods of our country is one of unchristian, immoral prejudice.

Sometimes morality demands that we go against convention. Jesus ignored the minute letter of the law in favor of the person. He was unconventional. So, frequently, are his followers: Francis of Assisi, Albert Schweitzer, Mother Teresa in India, and many, many others.

Should you feel the way you do? You didn't choose your feelings. It would be a great mistake to deny the way you feel. If you are tense and uncomfortable, then that's how you feel. The question is what to do about the feelings.

You feel that you have failed and that perhaps your daughter is rebelling. Yet she says she will give up her boyfriend rather than be disowned. Your daughter apparently cares deeply about a young man. She also cares deeply about her family. She hardly sounds rebellious. Our heart goes out to a young woman who must choose between her boyfriend and her family simply because of distrust against people of another color.

You don't want her to make a mistake she will regret the rest of her life. What is the mistake? Is marrying a black man the mistake? Is giving up the man she loves a mistake?

Your daughter is an adult. At this point she is probably having great difficulty with this decision. There is no easy answer. If she herself has difficulty knowing what is best, how can you or anyone else know what is best for her?

What can you do? First, although this is difficult because it goes against your own convention, tell yourself firmly that your daughter is doing nothing wrong.

Second, recognize your feelings and tell them to your daughter honestly. Some things which you might tell her are: "I feel tense; I know that's my problem. I want what is best for you. I'm afraid if you marry this man, you'll have many problems, perhaps more problems than you can handle." This is very different from saying, "Don't marry this man."

Third, if you love her, support her. Recognize the difficult choice she has. Tell her you will support her even if the decision she makes is different from the one you would make.

Finally, pray for her and the young man. Pray that their decision is wise. And while you are praying, pray for our country wherever the immoral attitude of prejudice blights our lives. Prejudice is immoral. Love between a white woman and a black man is not.

# Driving Privileges

**Our 16-year-old son will be getting his driver's license soon. I would like some suggestions about letting him use the family car. We have only one car, and we will have three drivers—my husband, myself and our son.**

Parents hold widely differing policies in regard to driving privileges for teens. Some parents never permit their children to drive the family car. If you want to drive, they say, earn and finance your own car. Other parents grant unlimited use of the family car or even buy a car for the child. Most parents fall somewhere between these two extremes.

The amount you let your son use the car is up to you. There is no right answer. You will probably maintain a smoother relationship if you spell out the policies early in his driving career.

Assuming you are going to share the family car, here are some of the points you need to consider:

*Who pays for insurance?* Insuring a teenage male is expensive. Your insurance company can give you the rate and can tell you how much of the total cost is due to having a teenage male driver in the family.

*Who pays for gas?* When this policy is not spelled out, everyone involved frequently feels cheated. Son thinks he puts in more than his share, and Dad feels he is always filling the empty tank that Junior left him. If this issue causes controversy, you can try a weekly assessment for your son or he can keep track of the miles he drives.

*How often can he have the car?* If this issue is not spelled out, your son might have to depend on your mood. When you feel good, he can have the car; if not, he can't. Such uncertainty can lead to resentment and frustration on his part. You might agree he can have the car one night per week, or whenever he gives you a day's notice. Obviously, emergencies and family needs supersede his claim, but having a policy can avoid a lot of resentment.

*Where can he go?* Must he let you know where he is taking the car? May he leave town? Must he let you know if he is leaving town? Such questions arise in a mobile culture such as ours.

*What about drinking and driving?* Are there special penalties for this very serious offense?

*Will taking away the use of the car ever be used as a punishment?* If so, will this punishment be used for any offense or only for abuse of driving privileges?

There are also some problems to anticipate: Who pays in the event of an accident? Who pays if he gets a ticket? Are there any penalties from you for getting a ticket? For getting stopped by the police?

Asking all these questions may seem to be making too much of a simple privilege. However common it may be in our country, driving a car is a privilege involving a lot of money and a lot of responsibility. Anticipating the problems and talking them over with your son can alleviate many controversies and misunderstandings.


# Religious Education

I read with great interest your column telling of your teens' resistance to formal emphasis on religion and moral problems. Maybe my kids aren't abnormal after all.

My question: Have you any materials we could use or could you direct us to some author who offers a "how to" on going about discussing dreams, feelings, interests and frustrations with teens?

We have been gathering with several other families for

the past two years in our parish's family-centered religious education program. It has been good, but we've encountered much resistance from our teens. I don't think these programs really can work for families with teens.

As your letter illustrates, religious education for teens is not easy. No one to our knowledge has come up with a sure-fire attractive program. Thank you for sharing your insights that small group programs, which work well for families with younger children, are still not popular with teens.

While we wish we could offer you a step-by-step, how-to program, we have none. We can only offer two guidelines which we think are crucial and then discuss some of our own family experiences which we consider moderately successful.

First, the guidelines: We think that teens resist any prepared program that is handed to them with the implication, "You will like this." Second, we think teens participate in family and parish much like the rest of us, that is, when they sincerely feel that they, as young adults, are important and necessary.

Next, our experience: We have family night for about an hour every Sunday evening. All from seventh grade up are invited. We rarely discuss a formal religious or moral question. We do have an atmosphere where we enjoy each other's company and we feel free to talk. Parents usually plan the evening, but everyone offers suggestions.

Some evenings we play games, expressive games like charades or silly games like Pit. Sometimes we watch old family movies together or look at family albums. Designing a family album would make a wonderful family activity, but in our family, Dad, the custodian of the albums ever since our wedding, does this task beautifully.

Are these activities religious? Not directly. But they establish an atmosphere, a way of saying, "This is us." Within this sense of family all kinds of values—religious and otherwise—get communicated.

Some evenings we share a poem or record. One night we listened to a Robert Frost record. Another evening we had a play reading. Since we are Neil Simon fans, we chose *The Odd Couple*. We find that roommates frequently resemble those characters. Letting roommates play these parts added special hilarity to the evening.

These evenings are successful, we think, because we never plan activities to educate, elevate, or preach. We choose things we truly want to share. When we have a moral or religious discussion, we discuss a problem which puzzles us.

Other evenings our science-minded children have shared their knowledge of pulsars, black holes and the expanding universe. These ideas led into a discussion of our concept of God. God does not change, but will the concept of God for a space-age people be vastly different from that of an agrarian people?

We have developed our programs according to our interests, which, we think, is the only way to realize success. If you have fewer than five discussants in your family, you might want to invite other teens and adults to join you.

If your family tries some ideas you enjoy, we would like to hear about them. Perhaps when many families have tried and shared ideas, we will develop some good general programs. For the most part, however, we think each family must develop and adapt ideas according to their own needs and interests.


# Church Attendance

**My teenager has stopped going to Mass. He doesn't seem to have any negative feelings about the Church; he just doesn't see the point. I want my son to enjoy the comfort and support the faith has given me. What can I do?**

Looking at how one Christian group, the Bruderhof, treats their teenage children can help us put our own concerns about teens and faith development in context.

The Bruderhof is a Christian community whose members share all their worldly goods and strive to live the gospel throughout every day of their lives. This commune is no group of college kids, but a movement which began in 1920 and whose members are third- and even fourth-generation members of the community. The group numbers around 750 men, women and children living in three colonies in New York, Pennsylvania and Connecticut.

The Bruderhof takes literally the idea that Christians should be in the world but not of it. The people live, work, worship and play together. While guests are welcome, they are expected to join in the life, including work, if they stay more than a day or two. Bruderhof members do not join clubs or organizations outside of the community. The children do not play with outside children. The children are educated at the community school by certified teachers who are members of the Bruderhof.

While the Bruderhof keeps adult members and children isolated from the world, teenagers are treated completely differently. The high schoolers attend the local public high school. After high school teens are encouraged, even prodded, to establish contact with the outside world. They go to college or take jobs on the outside.

There seems to be a contradiction between the attitude toward adults and children and the attitude toward teens. The Bruderhof explains it thus: Adults are members because they have chosen this way of life. Children are members because they have not yet reached the age of choice. But teenagers are not members of the community in the same sense. Teenagers are in transition. The Bruderhof is most concerned that Bruderhof children do not drift into the community because it is the path of least resistance. Thus they make it hard for them to join the community and easy for them to go out into the world. The fact that the community has third and fourth generation members indicates that many of the Bruderhof children do choose to come back.

The attitude of the Bruderhof is interesting for those of us who live in much more loosely-knit Christian communities as members of a Church. Often we are far less willing than the Bruderhof to let our children go off. We expect them to take part in Church activities just as they did when they were small children. And not infrequently, our children show us that they are in a period of transition. Like it or not, they choose values contrary to ours. Claiming that church has no meaning for them, they refuse to attend.

Parents faced with such behavior often conclude that they have failed. Yet the Bruderhof members, who demand far more commitment than we do, urge their teens to go off. Teens must view the outside world and choose their course in life. People who have followed the line of least resistance never make an adult choice for themselves. They are not valuable members of the community.

Letting children go is difficult and risky. Not all children who refuse to attend church are having a crisis of faith. Some of them may have had a very late Saturday night. But perhaps we other Christians can learn from the Bruderhof that, while letting go is risky, it is the only course. The teen who attends church because "my dad will kill me if I don't" is acting on the level of a young child. Unless he has the opportunity at some time to examine his life and to choose to follow Christ, he can never make an adult commitment to the Christian community.

# 'Grounding'

I am a 16-year-old girl. Last Saturday night I got in at 1 a.m., an hour later than my curfew. I was late for the second week in a row. My dad "grounded" me indefinitely, or as he put it, "until my attitude improves." I know I did wrong but I think the punishment is unreasonable. He said

**to write you. What do you think?**

We agree with you. We think you did wrong, but the punishment is unreasonable. The punishment is not unreasonable because it is too harsh, but because there are better ways to enforce curfew.

Sometimes we parents get so involved in exacting retribution that we forget what we started out to control. Punishment is only one part of discipline. Discipline means all the things we do to obtain desirable behavior from our children.

Your dad wants you home on time. It is important to keep a focus on this fact. "How do I get my daughter home on time?" is a different question from "How do I punish her for what she has done?"

There is no punishment that teens object to more than being grounded for an indefinite period. The teens we have talked with have the feeling they will never get out again. They are angry. They feel abused. They even think of running away (and sometimes do).

"Hurray!"says one set of parents. "We have finally found a way to put the fear of God into our teenager. Since she hates to be grounded, that is exactly what we shall do if she disobeys."

Unfortunately, grounding often does not work. The teen stays out late again. And is grounded again. And so it goes.

Why? Grounding lasts too long. Getting out of an indefinite sentence appears hopeless. The condition, "until your attitude improves," depends as much on dad's mood as it does on daughter's behavior. In such a situation breaking the rules again appears the only route to freedom.

Grounding also carries a peculiar kind of reward. Parent and teen talk endlessly about the curfew, the grounding, bad attitudes, and being freed. Dad pays far more attention to the "bad" daughter who is grounded than he would to a "good" daughter who followed the rules. Attention is rewarding even when it concerns bad behavior. Thus long, vague punishments actually reward bad behavior through attention.

One alternative you might suggest to your dad is household chores. Surely, your family has woodwork and windows to wash, a basement to clean or a yard to pick up. Suppose your dad grounded you until you did one hour's work for each half hour you were late. That way you can control how long the grounding will last.

Another important factor in discipline is to pay attention when things go well. Does your dad notice when you get home on time? Perhaps he could give you a check or a star every time you are home before curfew. Each star might be worth 15 minutes of extra "late" time. By getting home on time you could earn extra time to stay out late once in a while.

You will have learned to come home on time. When you fail, you can work it off to your parents' satisfaction. See what your dad thinks. We would welcome a letter from him.

# Drinking

**Last weekend my 17-year-old came home drunk at 3:00 a.m. He has never stayed out that late before, and he has never given us any trouble. The boys he pals around with seem to be nice boys. How should I handle him? What if it happens again?**

According to the laws in our society, 17-year-olds may not drink. The simplest solution may seem to be to follow the laws, forbid your son to drink, and punish him severely for drinking.

While this solution seems simple, we do not advise it for several reasons. First, you cannot enforce such a rule with a 17-year-old. He and his friends have access to cars. If they choose, they can get away from all adult supervision and drink. Even less can you enforce such a rule when a young man or woman is 18 or 20.

One of the main jobs of parenthood is to prepare a child for independence. In this case parents have the right and duty to teach a child about alcohol and drinking behavior. If he is going to learn to drink and make some mistakes in the process, it is far better he do so while he is at home than after he leaves home as a young adult. Teaching a child how to use alcohol is far more difficult than forbidding it, but it is the only approach which will help him in the next few years and throughout life.

In regard to last week's episode, listen to your son. Try to find out what happened, who he was with, where and how much he drank. If you explode in anger or set down punishments immediately, you will cut off all further communication.

Tell your son how you feel. Do you feel all drinking is wrong? Do you feel drinking is all right at times, but getting drunk is unacceptable? Try to share your own views and feelings.

Try to talk about some of the problems he faces as a teenager. Does he know how to drink one drink slowly so that he consumes very little over a period of time? How might he handle peer pressure when he is with a group of boys for whom being "one of the crowd" means getting drunk? You cannot answer these questions easily any more than your son can, but if you can talk together about them, you can help him clarify his own thinking.

Finally, formulate some guidelines regarding drinking. For example, here are the ones we use with our teens:

1) *Never drive when you drink.* If you drink even one beer, call parents for a ride home. It might be embarrassing, but it might keep you alive.

2) *No beer or liquor in the car ever.* Period. (For us, drinking and driving is the number one prohibition. Getting drunk won't kill you. Getting drunk and driving can kill you and some other innocent motorist you hit.)

3) *Set limits on how much you can drink,* for example, three beers. Keep track from the first drink. There is no point in trying to count after you are too fuzzy to remember. Trust your limits and stick to them. Do not think you can add a few more because you don't seem to feel anything from what you have drunk so far.

4) *You may drink at home.* Your friends may drink at our house provided we have talked with their parents and the parents know and approve. Your friends may not drive afterwards. They may stay all night at our house, or we will drive them home. Drinking with friends applies to an occasional weekend evening and a modest amount. We are not talking about a daily occurrence or about getting drunk.

5) *Coming home drunk will carry a penalty* spelled out in advance.

Will these guidelines make your son a wise, sensible drinker? They will help. Growing up is rough, and there are setbacks. He may come home drunk again, and you will have to enforce whatever penalty you have established. The importance of setting guidelines is to spell out clearly what is acceptable and what is not. Persons who have learned how to handle alcohol are less apt to become alcohol abusers. Guidelines help him chart a path in dealing with a new situation, drinking behavior.

# Drugs

Our 15-year-old son is breaking our hearts. We see him come home high on pot almost every night. His school work is going downhill. Two weeks ago the school phoned us to say they suspected he and a few friends smoke pot on the way to school. At the time I refused to believe it.

Two nights ago Dad looked around Jeff's room and found some pipes and cigarette papers and a sandwich bag with some crumbly brown material that we guess was marijuana.

Dad destroyed it, of course.

Last night Jeff came home glassy-eyed and a bit shaky. Dad confronted him. Jeff yelled back and ran out of the house. He did not come home again till this morning.

This is a very hard letter for me to write. I don't want to admit that my son has a drug problem. Where did we go wrong? And even more important, what do we do now? I feel so helpless and inadequate.

Thank you for your eloquent letter. In reaching out to ask for help, you have taken a big first step. Families of teenagers need community support. It is not easy to raise teenagers in our culture.

We agree with you that Jeff has a drug problem. Whatever one says about marijuana, Jeff's use of it has reached the point where it is interfering in some significant ways with his home life (your expectations of him) and his school performance.

We do not agree with you in assuming that Jeff's use of pot is the result of bad parenting. As a teenager, Jeff is vulnerable to many influences in our culture. His agemates, advertising and the pleasurable mellowing effect of pot on his mind can all act to overcome the very best of parenting.

Although you feel helpless at present, you may have more resources than you realize. Do you have any relatives with whom Jeff might stay for a short time? A grandparent? Aunt or uncle? One who has licked a drug or alcohol problem would be especially good. A simple, temporary time out may serve to restore the balance between you and Jeff.

How about Jeff's friends? Have you ever thought of inviting them over and listening to them? Almost certainly Jeff smokes with his companions, and they are an important key to the how, when, where and why of it. We have never met any young people who did not possess some redeeming qualities—virtues like loyalty, generosity and cleverness. Listen to Jeff's friends. You do not have to accept their pot smoking in order to learn more about it and them.

"Big brothers" can provide a friend and model outside the family. A wise addictions counselor can often talk straight to teenagers.

We have three suggestions for whomever relates to Jeff:

1) Be firm. Control what you can and lay off what you cannot control. Most parents start with evening curfews, a deadline to be home.

2) Don't judge. Allow Jeff his self-esteem. Without that he will never come back. Criticism and admonishment do more to break down than to build.

3) Be patient. God isn't finished with Jeff yet. Use your community resources to build a firm yet loving network. Then give it time.

# Marijuana

**My 16-year-old son smokes marijuana on an average of every other day. I am the one who caught him. Of course, I insisted that he stop. He told me, however, that marijuana was harmless. He says that he smokes it because it is a good way for him to get mellow and relax. He insists that he should be allowed to smoke in our home. His reasoning is that he will not get caught there.**

**My question: Is marijuana really harmless? I have heard so many different things about the subject that I really do not know what to think about it. But since I am faced with making a decision, I must have a definitive answer. I certainly do not want my son to continue something that may be harmful to him.**

Dr. Sidney Cohen of the Center for Health Sciences, the University of California in Los Angeles, chaired a panel of eight medical experts with divergent viewpoints on marijuana use. The experts agreed on eight positions. Recently they presented their findings to the House Select Committee on Narcotics Abuse and Control. Their findings were:

1) Young people should be discouraged from using marijuana.

2) Driving under the influence of marijuana can be hazardous.

3) Pregnant women should not use it.

4) Individuals with lung disease should avoid marijuana because of its irritating effects on the lungs.

5) Persons with heart disorders may be further impaired because of the increase in heart rate brought on by use of the drug.

6) Marijuana may precipitate a psychotic break in persons prone to schizophrenia.

7) Using marijuana less than once a week will probably not cause ill effects in adults.

8) The therapeutic potential of marijuana, particularly for managing nausea and glaucoma, should be studied further.

Marijuana use presents some clear dangers to the young, and its use should be discouraged. Better, and legal, ways to get mellow and relax can be found.

Why not suggest to your son that he study yoga? This is a wonderfully relaxing thing to do. Further, yoga helps to develop one's powers of concentration, and it's healthy.

As we discuss the question of marijuana, we are reminded of the fact that we adults (quite a number of us) use drugs that are known to have more serious side effects than marijuana. (It should be noted that marijuana is still being studied and we almost undoubtedly do not have all the answers yet.) Nevertheless, let's consider alcohol for a moment. Alcohol is a toxin. Then there are cigarettes. It's a proven fact that cigarette smoking can lead to lung disease, emphysema and cancer. Clearly this practice is dangerous to our health. Other drugs that are reported to be terribly abused are physician-prescribed tranquilizers like Valium and Librium. The side effects of these drugs are known to be more dangerous than the use of marijuana.

During the Prohibition era, large numbers of adults made whisky in their bathtubs. Again, this is probably a more dangerous drug than marijuana. It must be difficult for those particular adults to condemn the pot-smoking youth of today.

Let us discourage drug use among our youth by example, by cutting down on our tranquilizer and cigarette use and our consumption of alcohol. If we do not give them a good example, then we are guilty of hypocrisy when we criticize them for smoking pot.

It is really ridiculous to swallow anything that dulls our minds and harms our bodies. It is equally ridiculous to inhale anything into our lungs that either injures the lungs or affects our minds. Each of us has only one body and one mind. Ultimately, no one else can take the responsibility of keeping both mind and body healthy. That is something we have to do for ourselves. If we become ill in spite of looking after ourselves well, that is unfortunate. But if we deliberately abuse ourselves, we are inviting problems.

At any rate, let us teach our youth good health habits by setting a good example ourselves. Unless we do so, they are apt to ignore our advice with regard to things like marijuana and alcohol.

# Living Away

My 17-year-old daughter graduated in June and goes to college in September. She is working this summer, except on weekends. She wants to go in on a house at the shore with her girlfriends. I said it would be too loose and wild. I asked if they would be going to clubs, as most will be 18. Truthfully she said, "Yes, why not?"

I feel any drinking, especially unsupervised away from home, can lead to trouble or even an auto accident. She said I worry too much. Her father agreed. He said there is nothing we can do about it because she can leave home at 18, be on her own. What is a reasonable curfew after graduation? Please give me your advice for such situations, as we do have a wonderful relationship, open and honest.

If your child were 10 or 12, we might suggest: "Permit this because..." "Forbid that because..." Would that such simple directives could be given for young adults.

Your daughter is about to reach adult status. The law and society recognize this. Parents can no longer treat her like a child.

Instead let us address some basic questions: What are your short-term goals for the next year or so? What are your long-term goals? What relationship do you want with your adult daughter? What kinds of behavior can you require of an adult child?

Your concerns indicate that in the short-run you want your daughter safe, alive and out of trouble. In the long run, let us suppose that you want the honest relationship you now enjoy.

You could support her in living away from home this summer, or you could forbid it. Since your daughter consulted you openly and honestly, you may well be successful either way.

Suppose you forbid her to live away this summer. Apparently she will agree, but she will be angry and may or may not leave for good when she is 18. In any case, you will face the same situation in September when she goes to college. Then she will decide where she goes and what time she comes home.

Suppose you agree with her plan for the summer. You realize the dangers. These problems are less likely to occur if your daughter lives at home. But they affect every young adult. You cannot keep your daughter from drinking or from an auto accident by keeping her home. (Our 17-year-old son who had not been drinking had a head-on collision in the rain at midday. He walked away. We were lucky.)

There are advantages to letting your daughter pursue her plan. The summer can be a sort of trial run for college. She will be on her own but within short range of home. If you treat her as an adult she will face adult responsibilities. She must pay her rent, buy and prepare her food, do her wash. Opportunities for wild living will be limited by time and money. Most high-school graduates cannot make enough money to support their basic needs and still have a lot left. She might find that independence involves more drudgery than she supposed. Whether at home or at the shore, we think young adults should set their own hours once they graduate from high school. This recognizes adult status and prepares them for life away from home.

Supporting your daughter's plan is not doing nothing. Support offers greater opportunities to keep a good, open relationship. If she feels support rather than criticism, she is likely to stay close to you during the summer, to share her experiences and problems. You may be able to help her prepare for living on her own at college.

# College—Or What?

**My husband and I are "sick" because our son doesn't plan to go to college. He will graduate this coming June with a B-plus average. He says he's tired of school. He also refuses to make any other plans. Please help us.**

Frankly, let him alone at this point for several reasons. If you force him into college, he probably won't do well anyway. A great many young people with adequate intelligence fail in their first year or two of college because they don't apply themselves. Parental pressure is not enough to convince a student to study hard.

Then, too, a college degree is not as valuable as it was 10 years ago. The white collar jobs are filled. The job openings are in the skilled technical areas. Yet these skills are probably best learned on the job or at a technical school. A college degree may give one status, but there are other ways to acquire knowledge and higher salaries.

It sounds as though your son is not ready to profit from college. He may be right when he says he is tired of school. He may need to knock around in the real world for a while to find some life goals for himself.

Eighteen is now the age of majority. Our culture considers him old enough to sign contracts, get married, vote, die for his country. I think he is old enough to make his own decision about college.

There are many ways to learn. Travel is a special kind of education. Some young people learn a great deal from a year of "bumming around." Unskilled jobs are also valuable. You can meet some fascinating people building roads or working for a fast-food service. The hardest working college students we know are those who have let some time lapse between high school and college.

Obviously you are worried that if he doesn't go to college immediately after high school graduation, he may never go. That is certainly a possibility. But then, college isn't everything. If, on the other hand, he does return to school, he will return as a more mature student. In any case, we think it must be his decision.

Be patient. The values you have taught him as a growing child will emerge in time. This is not the moment to force them. We would support him in any reasonable life plan in which he shows an interest. Give him the same vote of confidence that our laws do when they proclaim him an adult. This does not mean that he will make no mistakes, but he is now free to choose.

# Professional Help

My 14-year-old son, eldest of three children, has been somewhat difficult. He was hyperactive in elementary school and now is sullen and uncooperative.

He can be sensitive and loving and has a sense of humor, but none of this has shown up much lately. Educated in a Catholic elementary school, he did not get along well there. After a dreadful eighth grade, we decided to move him to a public school. He found it difficult to make friends there and I'm sure he was lonely.

He now has a friend at school and life seems a little easier for him. His marks have improved slightly. Tests by a psychologist showed superior ability.

The school psychologist suggested counseling. But after a few visits he decided he didn't need it. He says he won't go any more.

He had a job mowing lawns which he quit. He couldn't get along with his customers. He got a job delivering groceries, but said he was fired for losing some. I found items I am sure he had stolen from the grocery store. Later he had episodes of stealing money from family members.

He plays his music very loud so that we are after him to turn it down. I drew up a contract with him to try to regulate this music, stating times when he could play it loud. After a few weeks he tore up the contract and threw it away.

Each of our children has a weekly job. He usually forgets his, does it angrily and says I nag him.

He gets on reasonably well with his brother, but fights break out because he takes things from his brother's room. He doesn't get along with his sister.

He hasn't participated in any sports this year, though he played baseball every year before.

My husband tries hard and assists him with his homework. But sometimes the going gets tough and my husband blows his top.

**I would value any advice you can offer.**

You have detailed a common parent-child problem with interaction. The description you give and the concern you show suggest you have made a maximum effort. Your son seems intent on resisting you.

Fourteen is a difficult age. The person is in transition between childhood and adolescence, between family and peer values. People are most apt to resist change of any kind in this phase.

However, things are likely to get worse as the problems of adolescence—curfews, alcohol, drugs, sex—become more serious. We think you should change your strategy.

Counseling for your son is not enough. One or two hours per week will not help him change. You are the ones who need help, either child guidance or family counseling. You sound like very good parents, but we think you need to become exceptional parents.

Although the problem does not appear to be your fault, you are the ones who need to become the agents of change.

One thing is obvious. Frontal attacks lead to resistance. The more you help with homework, the more you encourage employment, the more resistant he becomes. You need to find another way to promote success in these areas.

We suggest focusing on a few behaviors which are most important to you and attempt to encourage these "good" behaviors in positive ways. You must understand what rewards and motivates him. Ideally you need to find a system which rewards him for behavior that is desirable to you.

Bad behavior, like stealing, has consequences. Be careful not to protect your son from these consequences.

Consult some trusted friends who seem to be doing well with their adolescents. Or seek a mental health or family guidance clinic to help you improve skills.

You have a difficult discipline problem. You need an approach that will be less resisted. Good luck!

# Eighteen and Beyond
# Adult Children

When are parents no longer responsible for their children?
What about adult children who are dating divorced persons?
Living with someone without being married? Drinking too
much? Suffering through an unhappy marriage? What about
rules for adult children who are still living at home? We have
one guideline which has some very useful applications: We
should treat our adult children the same way we treat our
dearest and best friends.

149

# Who's Responsible?

Please answer a few important questions:

1) How long are we as parents responsible for our children's actions?

2) Would I be right or wrong to search my 19- and 20-year-olds' drawers for filthy porno books—even birth control pills? Maybe everybody is doing it, but that doesn't make it right. I've always felt as long as they have their feet under our table, we are responsible for them.

As parents we are responsible for teaching our children our values and those of our society, for disciplining them according to their age and experience, and for noticing and rewarding the good things they do. We are never responsible for our child in the sense of controlling behavior or thoughts. We are not responsible if our four-year-old Johnny kicks the 60-year-old gentleman next door, but we are certainly responsible for seeing that Johnny learns that this is unacceptable behavior and he had jolly well better not do it again.

With adult children—and 19- and 20-year-olds are adults—the opportunity to teach and discipline is over. We certainly cannot control their minds or their behavior. Thus we conclude that parents are *not* responsible for the actions of their adult children.

What if they do something wrong? We must recognize that they, and not we, are responsible for their behavior.

Since sexual mores are changing in our society, it is natural for parents to be most upset over these issues. We might get a better picture, though, if we take other examples. Suppose your working daughter cheats her employer by taking long lunch hours and long, long coffee breaks. Suppose your son sells a car for $500 which he knows is not worth $100. Suppose your child cheats on an exam. Are you responsible? Can you control this problem? It is unfortunate, but it is not your problem.

We must be careful not to try to play God with our children. God our Father lets us make terrible mistakes. He does not control our minds. We don't think he blames himself when we fail. (Incidentally, to carry the analogy further, he never stops caring for us, believing in us, or giving us another chance.) Surely, as parents, we should not be more controlling than God.

What about going through adult children's drawers? We wouldn't. We are not condoning porno books or your son's actions; however, what positive good is accomplished? You can destroy these books, but you cannot keep your son from buying and reading other books.

The same applies to birth control pills. You can destroy the pills, but you cannot control your daughter's ideas or behavior in regard to her sexuality.

On the negative side, you will destroy trust between you and your children. If you snoop once, your children will always suspect that you will do it again. Breaking trust is a high price to pay.

Personally we would not pay this high price unless we had reason to suspect that our child was involved in a robbery ring, was trafficking in hard drugs, was likely to kill another person, was pregnant and considering an abortion, or something similarly serious. In these extreme cases we consider the harm or potential harm against other human beings so serious it supersedes the child's (or anyone else's) right to privacy. In less serious cases we would value more the child's right to privacy and the trust between us.

Can you do anything? Certainly. You can set standards in your home over matters you can control. You can't control what is in your children's rooms without snooping. You cannot say, "You must believe that premarital sex is wrong." You can say, "I believe that premarital sex is wrong. In this house you may not have guests of the opposite sex stay overnight." You are not telling your adult children how to feel and act. You are expressing how you feel and act. You are giving an

"I-message." Your children will respect your honesty and integrity whether they agree with you or not.

Professionals and ordinary people agree that the values learned in the family are the most powerful influences on a child's life. Parents often must take this fact on faith. It sometimes seems that all our values have broken down. Trust that they haven't. Focus on the good things your young adults do, and don't blame yourself for matters you cannot control.

# House Rules

**Our 19-year-old daughter feels she should live her own life in her own way and has consequently stayed out all night a number of times. She fails to call and thus breaks a house rule of which she is aware. She told us she has stayed with a young divorced man and she does not feel premarital sex is wrong.**

**I cannot accept many of her values but realize she must make the decisions that determine her own value system. To what extent, however, should children over 18 living at home live by house rules, and under what conditions would it be fair to ask them to leave?**

Thank you for "telling it like it is." Your letter presents a vivid picture of conflict between parents and young adult children. You have already worked out many of your own answers. We shall merely summarize what you can and cannot do.

First, you cannot get inside her mind and change it to your liking. This you have discovered.

Second, you cannot control your daughter by emotional pressure. Examples of such attempts are: "You can't do that because I say it is wrong." "You can't do that because I won't love you if you do." This type of pressure does not work, and threats are alienating.

What can you do?

First, you can demand adult responsibility from any child who claims adult freedom. This means you can expect her to support herself financially and to contribute to the household both financially (perhaps $5 to $8 per day) and by doing chores. This also means you do not lend her money when she runs short of cash. You do not give her free room and board when she quits one job and does not find another. You do not give her free access to the family car. You do not cook, sew, iron and mend for her on demand.

Second, you can expect her to observe rules which are important to you. For example, you cannot forbid her to engage in premarital sex. Forbidding doesn't make it so. But you can say, "Your father and I are in charge of this house and this family. Staying out all night is so contrary to our values that we cannot be comfortable with such behavior in our home. The example you are setting before your younger brothers and sisters is against the principles your father and I believe in. For the sake of the family, you must come home every night or get your own place to live."

Third, you must decide how much you value maintaining family bonds—despite the intolerable behavior of your adult child.

When an adolescent child rejects our values and behaves contrary to our moral code, we parents often focus on the bad behavior until it becomes almost an obsession. Perhaps only parents of difficult adolescents can understand how all-consuming this obsession can become.

A parent's thoughts run something like this: "Every time I look at that girl I think of how she is defying all that I value. I am furious at her. She has upset any peace and order I had managed to secure in my life. I have loved and cared for her since birth. It is simply not fair of her to act this way. Sometimes I'm afraid she'll go off and never come back to us—and other times I wish she'd do exactly that."

The more you dwell on the bad behavior the farther

153

apart you grow. The circle is destructive. Think for a moment. No matter how bad her behavior, do you really want to drive your daughter away forever? Is any behavior worth cutting the ties between you permanently?

You can hardly expect an adolescent daughter to initiate a process of forgiveness, healing and reestablishing ties. You, the parent, must take steps necessary to break the destructive circle:

First, *stop judging*. Does telling her she is wrong or bad do any good? No, she will either defend herself or ignore you. Whether you are right or wrong does not matter. Criticizing her or telling her what to do does not work.

Now take the hard step. *Forget about her bad behavior and concentrate on her good behavior*. What does she do well? Does she sew, cook or clean house well? Does she play tennis, play a musical instrument? Is she a good big sister to her siblings, generous and loyal to her friends? Perhaps she lends them money or clothes or buys them records. You might not even approve of her specific kindness, but kindness it is. Recognize it.

Look for the good things. Perhaps you can get your husband interested in this approach. Help each other to stay positive. Write down the good things you think of. The more you bring her good points to mind, the more you will see her virtues rather than her faults.

Jesus loved people who had done things far worse than your daughter. His love was supportive, healing both body and spirit. Jesus brought out the best in people. He loved even people who were strangers to him. Can we do less with our own children whom we love in spite of all?

You can clarify the issues between you by specifying what adult freedom and adult responsibility mean. Then go one step further. Translate your love for your daughter into approval of the goodness in her. As difficult as that is, it might be the one thing that keeps your love relationship alive.

# Curfews

You have said, "Once a child is graduated from high school, we no longer set hours. The child is an adult and expected to be responsible for his or her own hours."

I found this didn't work with my 20-year-old son. Twice recently I awakened after 5 a.m. and he wasn't in yet. I do not mean to imply he was doing anything immoral, but I feel that since he is still living at our house, he should respect our moral code, which is to be in at a decent hour.

At some time we must accept our children as adults and grant them adult independence. When is this point?

Is it when they act the way we would act or want them to act? Obviously, this day will never come. We are raising people, not puppets.

Our own culture grants various adult rights and privileges from 16 onward. Many cultures have a rite of passage which clearly defines for everyone in the society when a person becomes an adult. The nearest ritual we have is graduation from high school. Most children have reached 18 by this time, and most adult rights are theirs. This is the best objective standard for our society.

Can we accept our children as adults while they still live at home? Parents might say, "As long as you live in this house, you will follow our rules." Such a position is justified for those rules necessary for the running of the household. Thus we believe parents can say to children of any age, "You may not flick cigarette ashes on the carpet, or put your feet on the damask sofa, or leave dirty dishes in the sink." Such rules apply at all ages. They enhance living together.

Other rules are by nature designed to control the child's behavior. "You must come in at midnight" is a behavior-controlling rule. Parents cannot justify behavior-controlling rules for adults. If such rules apply as long as the child lives at home, then parents are saying, "You cannot be an adult as long as you live at home." Many parents make such rules, and many children move out of the home for just this reason.

If you wish, you can justifiably make rules for your own convenience, such as, "I'm a light sleeper. When you come in at 4:00 or 5:00 in the morning, I wake up and cannot sleep the rest of the night. Therefore, in our house everyone comes in before midnight." Such a rule is for *your* good, not for the control of your son. If you state this position honestly, you realize that your son may well choose to move out in order to live as he wishes and has a right to. We hope you will understand and support him in such a choice.

# 'Living in Sin'

**Our 24-year-old daughter is now living with a divorced man. I don't know how to treat them. I feel that welcoming them into my home would imply that I condone the situation. I love my daughter so much, and I pray constantly for all of us.**

Our mail is filled with such letters from the parents of grown children. What should the family do? Condemn the children and refuse all communication? Lecture them about their scandalous behavior? Ignore the situation and welcome the children because they belong to the family first, last and always?

No one can tell another person the "right" answer in such complicated and heart-rending situations. We can consider some important issues:

First, how does a parent treat adult children?

Second, how do you respond to others who are apparently living in sin?

Third, as Christians, what special response is required?

Eugene Geissler, an experienced father, once wrote, "God doesn't have grandchildren." In reaching adult children, God no longer works primarily through parents. Yes, God entrusts parents with the job of raising children, but at some point they are raised. Children become adults, and adults are responsible for their own behavior. The choices they make are theirs.

Certainly parents still influence their adult children. All of us touch each others' lives, and all of us can reveal God's love and Word to one another. But parents are no longer the special guardians and guides of adult children.

How do you treat other adults who are "living in sin"— your boss, your neighbor, your cousin, your old college roommate? Do you refuse to speak? Do you lecture them? Do you ignore their living situation and extend friendship to them?

The way you treat other adults is one possible guideline as to how to treat your own adult children. It is not the only guide, nor is it a foolproof guide. The influence on younger siblings has not even been considered. However complex the issue, we think that our own children should be treated *at least* as kindly and warmly as we would treat other adults in similar circumstances.

Beyond the minimum, however, what response should we make as Christians to our grown children who have refused our values? Basically we have two options: to correct and admonish or to accept and love. The example we get from Scripture is mixed. Christ corrects and admonishes some; he accepts and loves others.

Perhaps the figure who most closely resembles our "sinful, scandalous" children is the Samaritan woman at the well (John 4:4-42). Several aspects of Christ's behavior are striking. First, he reached out to her. He started the conversation. Second, at no point did he lecture her or criticize her. He was unfailingly kind. Third, the conversation with Christ led the woman herself to acknowledge her behavior ("I have no husband").

Christ gives us an example of kindness and

communication. He did not break off a relationship because the woman was a sinner. He started one. Christ did not judge or lecture, yet his presence led the woman herself to acknowledge her behavior.

The last point is particularly important in dealing with our children. Repentance and conversion cannot be imposed by another person. They come from within the heart. And the best way to communicate the beauty and goodness of the Christian life is for us to live as Christians, to reach out to others as Christ did in kindness and love.

This is not to say that kindness on your part will lead to repentance and conversion on the part of your children—immediately or ever. Our personal knowledge and understanding are so limited. We do not know God's plan for us, for our children, or for the world. We do not know what person or what means God is trying to use to touch the hearts of our children. Perhaps those two people "living in sin" will somehow be a means of grace for each other. Perhaps this relationship will shake us parents out of pride and complacency to humility and an acknowledgement that we cannot make everything turn out the way we would like.

Our primary goal for our children is not a lovely wedding in the proper church with all legal documents in order. Our goal is conversion, *metanoia,* the changed heart of the person who responds to Christ. We cannot bring that about for another person. We can merely reflect as best we can the kindness and love toward others which Christ demonstrated.

# Dating the Divorced

**My daughter has a divorced boyfriend. She is 18; he is 27. I pointed out that if they fall in love she can't marry him; it would be better to discontinue the friendship. My daughter goes to Mass with us, listens to the sermon and knows the rules. She wants us to receive him. I fear that if we invite**

him to our home, she might think everything will turn out all right—that she could marry him if she wants to. How far does charity go?

You seem to realize you cannot order your daughter to behave a certain way. As an adult, her decisions, however unwise they appear to you, are her responsibility. But your daughter does not seem to be ignoring or defying you. The lines of communication seem open.

How might you communicate your position while still indicating that she, not you, is responsible for the decisions about her life? The worst way to approach your daughter would be with firm, absolute directives: "I know best. You are wrong. Listen to me." No matter who is right, such advice is doomed to fail.

Since the relationship between you and your daughter seems to be direct and open, you probably can best reach her by simple, open messages about your personal views and emotions. You need not pretend positive feelings you do not have.

Essentially you might want to say: "You are an adult and I recognize that you must make your own decisions about life. Right now I feel very concerned about your relationship with this man because I see a lot of future problems. I'll love you whatever you decide, but I hope you will think long and hard before going further with this relationship."

This expresses honestly: 1) your recognition of her as an adult; 2) your love and concern for her whatever she does; 3) your grave reservations.

Should you entertain this boyfriend? We do not think entertaining him would give your daughter the idea that her relationship is "all right." She knows your values. Deep down these values are hers too, because she has learned them from you. She might struggle to rationalize her relationship but, if she is at all honest, she recognizes your disapproval.

We do not know whether you should entertain the

159

boyfriend. One guideline you might use is: What would you do if the situation involved a good friend or a neighbor rather than your daughter? At the least, you probably want to do for your daughter's friend what you would do for people not as close to you.

Whatever you decide, you can be direct with your daughter. If you decide to entertain him, you might say something like: "I feel very uncomfortable inviting this young man. I feel you are getting deeper into a relationship which cannot work out well. But I shall make him welcome because he is your friend, we are your family, and you want us to get to know each other."

If you simply cannot be comfortable inviting him, tell her that: "I love you and I wish I could go along with you. At this point, I feel so strongly against this relationship that I simply cannot welcome your boyfriend to our house. I'm sorry."

You cannot tell your daughter what to do. The most you can do is emphasize the seriousness of the relationship she is getting into and urge her to take time and give it a lot of thought. You can best communicate this through open, direct messages which express, not condemnation of her, but love and concern.

# Homosexuality

Not long ago our only son, 26, had to have therapy because of emotional problems. From this, after long, agonizing sessions, he very reluctantly acknowledged that he is a homosexual. We had not the slightest inkling that this could be but, in spite of the shock, we have never held our love from him.

My husband and I have kept this information to ourselves, since this is what our son wishes. We have one other child, a married daughter with children. She and my son have always been close.

Should we continue to keep this to ourselves and consider it, as our son does, his personal problem, or should we risk telling our daughter and perhaps break down their existing good family relationship? Are there any reasons why she would have to know?

No, don't tell your daughter. From your letter, we can see no reason why you have an obligation to inform her of your son's homosexuality.

Are you worried that he might do something wrong with her children? There is no reason to presume that homosexuals have any greater tendency to abuse children than heterosexuals. Many persons with gay tendencies are quite able to keep their sexual tendencies to themselves.

Perhaps you are worried that your grandchildren will be influenced by their uncle. We don't really know, but most evidence suggests that homosexuality is not primarily learned through modeling after others. It may be at least partially genetic.

If your grandchildren should find out, they would be more likely to know their uncle simply as a person rather than thinking of him as gay. They could value his love and friendship without any inclination to copy his sexual preferences. It might be nice for them to learn that there are many good and moral people who have gay tendencies.

The inclination toward homosexuality is not a matter of choice. Few people choose or will it. It is there. It must be dealt with. Society does not help by condemning the homosexual. Much tolerance and acceptance is needed in this matter.

We do not condemn people for tendencies that they cannot help. Freud himself wrote that this was one area that psychology and psychiatry were unsuccessful in treating. Homosexual *behavior* may be immoral, but certainly homosexual *tendencies* are not.

At a later time your son may want to inform his sister

about his sexual preferences. Most gays ultimately feel more comfortable when such information is out in the open. This must be your son's decision, however, and the initiative is up to him.

# Good Grandmothering

**In two months our daughter-in-law is due to give birth to our first grandchild. I'm planning to go to their home and help out for the first week or two. You are great supporters of relatives helping each other. Any suggestions about how to be a good grandmother?**

Dana Raphael, an anthropologist, studied child care and breastfeeding in several cultures. In her book *The Tender Gift,* she notes that many cultures provide the new mother with a *doula,* a person to "mother" the young mother. The *doula* takes care of anything that might bother the mother, leaving her free to get acquainted with her baby in a peaceful, secure atmosphere.

Our culture frequently expects the young mother to go it alone. She is expected to take up normal duties almost as soon as she gets home from the hospital. She is to cook, clean, even entertain, and still learn to know and mother her baby. Like all Americans, she is prized if she is efficient.

The young mother's main task in the early weeks is to get acquainted with her baby and learn to meet its needs with confidence. She needs peaceful, unhurried time with her baby.

A helpful grandmother's most likely mistake is to take over the baby, supposedly to give the mother time to rest. This temptation is hard to resist.

The good grandmother is enthusiastic about her grandchild. She agrees that this is the most marvelous baby ever. She recognizes, however, that her role is to support the mother. Here are some practical ways:

1) Encourage the new mother. Point out how well the baby eats, how contented it is. If the baby is fussy, do not add to the mother's concern but try to assure her. Do not insist on your way when her way is as good. If she uses paper diapers and you prefer cloth, if she feeds on demand and you think babies should eat on schedule, don't force your opinion. Such decisions are hers. What difference do they make so long as mother and baby are happy?

2) Take care of necessary tasks such as the wash and cooking. Freeing the new mother from those demands is the greatest practical help you can give her.

3) Find out the new mother's feelings about phone calls and guests. Congratulations add to the family's happiness, but some guests overstay their welcome. If she has too many visitors, deal with them tactfully.

4) Support her especially on "down" days. The happiest, healthiest new mothers have days when they get tired and easily upset, when everything seems to go wrong. If you give her plenty of time to rest, see that she eats well and stay calm and supportive, you can be a great asset.

5) Enjoy that grandchild. Letting the young mother learn how to mother does not mean you must never touch the baby. Hold and rock it to your heart's content. Bathe and dress the baby occasionally if the mother welcomes your help. You cannot spoil a baby. Most newborns like to be held whenever they are awake. There is plenty of time for both the mother and other family members to enjoy the baby.

Your role demands maturity. Your experience will stand you in good stead. If you do your job well, you will aid your daughter-in-law, you will help your grandchild to a wonderful start in life and you may develop a closer, warmer relationship with your son and his family than you would ever experience otherwise.

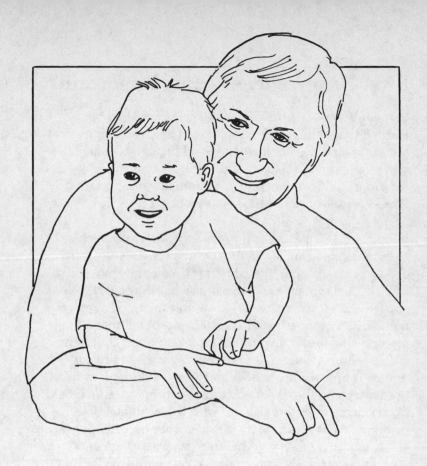

# Adoption

Despite the shortage of available babies today, adoption has received a new emphasis. Adoption provides a family resource for the hard-to-place or handicapped child. Adoption also needs careful consideration as an alternative to abortion. Parents are concerned about how to tell their child of his or her adoption. Other issues include how to go about adoption of hard-to-place children, and questions from both sides about the secrecy which separates the adopted child from the biological mother who originally gave him up.

# First Experiences—How Important?

In reading about the mother-child relationship, I have learned that bonds form very early in life, even in the first few hours or days. My husband and I hope to become adoptive parents. What are the implications for us? What if we adopt a one- or two-year-old child? How important are those very early experiences with a baby?

Infancy is a fascinating and popular topic. While much research is going on, few definitive answers can be given about babies. After all, it is difficult to communicate with babies. They cannot report in words what they are thinking and feeling. Moreover, babies grow and change so rapidly that we cannot make general statements about them. The newborn and the six-month-old infant are vastly different.

Researchers have found that when mothers are not drugged at birth, and consequently are awake and aware of the experience, they frequently form a dramatic attachment, experiencing a "falling in love" with their infants. Both mother and baby want to be together; they experience peace and tranquility when together and unease and unrest when separated even for brief periods. The popular term for this experience is *bonding*. Some researchers have correlated a positive bonding experience with a good mother-child relationship years later.

At the same time, research on infants offers very few answers about what experiences produce long-term effects and under which circumstances these effects occur. There are so many variables in human life that we must be cautious about absolute statements.

Some of the more positive findings from infant research are these:

1) There are many positive and good ways for an adult to relate to an infant. Studies show that mothers spend more time feeding babies; fathers spend more time playing with

babies. When they play with babies, fathers are rougher and more boisterous. Mothers do more talking, using words, stories and imagination. Lucky is the infant who experiences both!

2) Babies seem to be resilient. Each new experience is an opportunity for a new beginning. For example, if the baby is very fussy and colicky, the mother may feel that the feeding experience does not go well. Playing, holding, bathing, however, are also means of relating and they may be going very well.

There is another aspect of infant resilience. Stresses, even severe stresses, for a short period of time do not seem to have long-term damaging effects.

3) The most important single factor in child development seems to be the sensitivity of the mother to the child. When a mother is responsive and sensitive to her child, the child is likely to develop well along intellectual, social and emotional lines.

What does all this mean for you and for others who might be contemplating adoption or foster care? From what we know now we can say:

1) Nothing has been found that is fixed forever or lost forever due to mother-child bonding in the first few hours or days.

2) Infants are resilient; good relationships can be built in many ways.

3) An infant born into a difficult situation or a deprived background is not thereby scarred hopelessly for life; short stresses apparently can be handled, even by an infant.

4) Whether you begin mothering by giving birth, by adopting a newborn or by parenting a toddler, the single most important thing you can do for your child's development is to be a sensitive parent. Sensitivity simply means paying attention to, responding to and enjoying that child. In short, recent research, far from reducing the importance of good mothering, has found it to be crucial.

# Telling the Child

A number of years ago I married a woman who had a young daughter. After our marriage I adopted the child legally. My wife and I have just had a child of our own. The problem is we never told the older child that I am her father by adoption. Now she is seven and I think she should know. How do I tell her?

Every adoption is a love story. More than that, every adoption is a romance because romance may be defined as love plus adventure. That is adoption: love plus adventure.

There are actually two questions to deal with in your situation. The first is to sort out your own feelings about your daughter. Particularly in your case, where your wife is the biological mother but you are not the biological father, you may well feel, "I'm not the real father, only the adoptive father." Not so. The courts have given you full legal custody of your daughter. She has all the rights and privileges of a biological child—permanently. She is your daughter. You are not her biological father but you are her "forever father."

Helen Doss, an adoptive mother who has written extensively on adoption, remarks that she feels a legal hearing to finalize an adoption is much like a marriage ceremony. As the court hearing proceeds, she says to herself silently, "I take this child for better, for worse, for richer, for poorer, in sickness and in health until death."

Once you think through your feelings, many "problems" about adoption are clarified. You are free to discipline your daughter and to love her. You need not and should not relegate affection or discipline to your wife because she is the "real" parent. You are both the real parents. Moreover, with this thought firmly in mind, you need not be shaken when thoughtless people remark, "She's not your own child, is she?" This is an opportunity for you to state that both children are truly yours.

Having a biological and an adopted child is like having "cradle Catholics" and converts within the Church. Sometimes a subtle prejudice arises which implies that cradle Catholics are "better." In fact, both are fully members of the Christian community, and both enrich the community in their own ways.

When you understand your own feelings about adoption, you will find it much easier to tell your daughter. You are somewhat at a disadvantage because seven is rather old to hear the story of adoption for the first time. Two principles, however, apply to you or to any adoptive parent:

1) *Be informal.* Do not plan a special "adoption-telling session." For a seven-year-old such a session could easily imply that something secret and scary and bad was taking place. Instead choose a natural, intimate family setting: around the dinner table, bath time, or bedtime are obvious choices.

2) *Be positive.* Build on the idea that you have a romance to share—a story of love and adventure. Give details. What did she look like when you first saw her? What did she wear? What was she doing? Emphasize how much you wanted her for your little girl and how happy you were to become her "forever father." Emphasize the permanence and security of your relationship.

Do not worry if you omit some details on the first telling. Keep the subject open from now on. Add details and answer your daughter's questions when they come up. And always be positive in sharing with your daughter the wonderful story of how you all became one family.

# Why Secrecy?

Currently there is much interest and controversy over the question: Should adopted persons upon reaching adulthood have access to confidential records regarding their biological parents? Organizations have been formed in many states on both sides of the issue.

Frequently those who feel hottest on either side of this issue are those for whom adoption was kept a "secret" through most of childhood. The unspoken message from the adoptive parents was: Adoption is a secret, shameful stigma. Under such circumstances it is no wonder a person searches desperately for biological roots in order to find self-acceptance and a sense of dignity before others.

As parents of both biological and adoptive children, the secrecy surrounding adoption baffles us. We have always thought of adoption as a beautiful experience both for parents and child. You are no worse—and no better—than anyone else because you are adopted. Self-worth comes from inside.

Based on this attitude adoption stories constitute a rich part of our family lore. We show home movies of baby Michael coming home from the hospital and of baby Matthew coming home from the adoption agency. We tell bedtime stories about when Bitta was born and when Annie came to us from Canada to be a Kenny. Sometimes adoption seems almost too attractive. Once, when Annie and Bitta were small, we told about bringing Annie home on the jet plane. Bitta pouted, "When am I going to be 'dopted?"

We joke about adoption. When Annie told us about another girl in her class who is adopted, she remarked, "Her mother buys her anything she wants." Answered Mother, "Annie, why couldn't you be lucky and get into a family like that instead of getting stuck with us?"

Outsiders frequently distinguish between biological and adopted children. A common question is, "Which ones are really yours?" Although the question irritates us, we politely answer, "They all are." We realize the questioner is not unkind, simply thoughtless. In fact, adoption, more than any other parental experience, has taught us a profound lesson: Our adopted children are not ours. But neither are our biological children. In both cases we are entrusted with a special kind of stewardship. But *stewards* we are. They belong to themselves, and their independence is our goal.

Telling so many stories about adoption may make it appear that we are highly conscious of adoption. Actually we are rather matter-of-fact. Recently nine-year-old Bob had a friend visiting who had raised some questions. Bob asked his 13-year-old brother, "Pete, how many kids in our family are adopted?"

"Four," answered Peter.

"Which ones?" asked Bob.

The conclusion might be that Bob is blind (three of our children are biracial), stupid (we have told him many times) or threatened by the notion of adoption. I suspect all three notions are wrong and Bob has simply absorbed the easy-going family attitude.

Adoption is like birth. In some ways it is the singular most important event of your life. On the other hand it happens every day and is not something to brood about endlessly.

Adoption is a dramatic example of the human family in action. And the implication that it is second-rate is an insult to the Creator who has himself made us his children—by adoption.

# Rights of 'Biological' Parents

**I put up a baby girl for adoption in 1976. Is there any way my little girl can know who the real mother is? And when she gets older, does she have the right to see her mother?**

For a long time the philosophy of adoption agencies and courts has been to prevent the biological parent from coming in contact with the adopting parents or with the child. In response to adults who were adopted as children and to biological parents, that philosophy is now changing.

Currently many states are struggling to fashion laws which will respect the rights of the adopted person, the adoptive parents and the biological parents. The law varies considerably from state to state.

Let's start with your last question first. When your daughter attains age 18 or adult status, she surely has the right to seek you out. The usual procedure is for her to notify her local welfare department of her desire to locate you. It will contact the agency where the adoption took place and find out your name and last address. If and when it locates you, before giving her your address, you would be asked if you would like to hear from your daughter.

If your adult daughter felt the adoption agency were uncooperative, then she would want to hire a lawyer to press for the court records which would help her identify and find you. A very practical thing you might do in the meantime would be to make sure the agency and court involved in the adoption always have your current address.

Not every adopted child wants to see the biological parent. Some biological parents would prefer no further contact with the children they have given for adoption. Any further communication would be too painful for them.

Generally the role of the adoption agency and courts is to act as an intermediary, arranging for contact where both the parent and the child want it. If one party is unwilling, then the information may be kept confidential.

There are two kinds of parents: biological parents and forever parents. The biological parents conceive the child, and the biological mother nurtures the baby for nine months.

The forever parents take over at or shortly after birth. They provide the love, discipline, training and education, and they work to develop good habits. They need a free hand and complete responsibility in this task.

For most children, the biological parents and the forever parents are identical. Adoptive children are luckier in a way. They have two sets of parents. Contact between these two sets of parents is rare, however. Frequently, unlike yourself, the biological mother does not wish it. Just as often, the forever parents do not want it.

If you would like to establish contact with your daughter before she becomes an adult, we suggest you contact the agency which placed your child. It can inquire through channels whether the adopting parents are agreeable. If they are, fine. If not, we would urge you to respect their wishes since they are now the ones with the primary responsibility.

One thing you might do if they refuse contact is to write your daughter a letter or send a gift. The agency might be willing to pass it along to the adopting parents who may accept it to give to the child if and when the time is appropriate.

Your love for your absent child is commendable. You must extend that love to accept the fact that contact with your daughter may be delayed or even denied. Reach out to her in your thoughts and prayers.

# Rights of 'Forever' Parents

I am the mother of an adopted child. When I read about biological parents seeking out the children they placed for adoption, I feel very confused and hurt. I raised a child that I love, that is one of the most important things in my life.

How would the biological parent know the love that is shared in the sickness and hurts, being there every time the child needed me? Raising a child takes love and discipline, and I have given both.

Take my right arm, but let me keep my child. This child never once mentioned he would like to see his biological parents, but comments like yours plant ideas in his mind. I am sure he will become confused, too. I hope parents with adopted children will take a stand. Leave well enough alone.

Thank you for expressing so well how some adoptive parents feel. We too are adoptive parents. Four of our 12 children came to us through adoption. Then, three years ago, our unmarried daughter became pregnant and chose to give her child up for adoption. We experienced some of the love and anguish a biological mother feels entrusting her baby to another.

Like it or not, adoption involves a triangle: the biological parents, the adoptive parents and the child. All these people have needs.

Today in our society abortion is common and socially acceptable. The young woman who has a child and gives it up for adoption must be courageous. Such courage is becoming increasingly rare. She often has very little support from others, and her needs have often been ignored.

The "forever" parents are the "real" ones, the ones who have the responsibilities and make the decisions about what is good or bad for the child. Consequently, we have always said that any communication from the biological mother should be through the "forever" parents, based on their prudent judgments about what would be good for the child and the family.

As the "forever" mother, the adopted child is yours. We hope you can see the biological mother of your child, not as a threat, not as someone who is about to appear and take your child away, but as someone who has done you a service without measure or price. She has given you her child. Recognize the great gift she has given you. Bless her and pray for her.

If your child inquires at some time about his biological heritage, he is not rejecting you but is asking about an important part of his life. Curiosity about his heritage is normal. If he questions you, he shows that he trusts you enough to go to you for answers. *We* have not put these ideas in his head, and silence on the subject will not make his curiosity go away.

Sometimes an adopted child will tell the parents that he wishes they had never adopted him. Such talk may be a normal expression of adolescent frustration and rebellion. Both adopted and biological adolescents express these strong dissatisfactions at times. Try to understand that curiosity and frustration with parents are normal parts of growing up.

We fully agree with you that you have given the nourishment, the support, the love, discipline and tears that it takes to be a parent. You are the "forever" parent. Be confident of this fact. Any challenges from your child or from the outside world are not denials that you are truly the parent. They are merely problems to be worked out in the best and most loving way.

# Should We Adopt?

**My husband and I are childless after eight years of marriage, and we have been thinking about adoption. I really would like to have children, but I feel some reservations about adoption. I'm afraid I might not love an adopted child like I would my own. Do you think I should pursue the idea of adoption or just forget it?**

Mixed feelings about adoption are not at all unusual. We have mixed feelings about any major decision which is going to change the course of our lives: career, marriage and, certainly, children. Furthermore, being childless and wanting children is a situation which can cause deep feelings.

These feelings are hard to face in oneself and even harder to discuss with someone else. When a couple already has children, they wonder whether they will love adopted children "just like" they love their biological children. Certainly all couples contemplating adoption wonder, as one prospective adoptive mother put it on the way to pick up her first child, "What if I don't like him?"

If your mixed feelings about adoption resemble the feelings you had before choosing a career or getting married, they are probably the normal feeling that go with making hard decisions. It might be helpful to find someone to talk with about childlessness. Most friends with children find it difficult to understand this problem, but any close friend or relative who is a good listener might help you think out and talk about your own feelings.

Trying to love children "all alike" is, we think, a wrong goal for both biological and adoptive parents. Children are not all alike. Each one is unique in personality, talents, looks, responses. Parents cannot program or direct their feelings to treat all their children alike without falsifying those feelings. This is not to say that parents should respond to the child they find most attractive and feel free to ignore the less attractive child. What we are suggesting is that every child can be loved for his or her own uniqueness.

When the child's interests and talents are similar to those of the parent, it is easy to respond to and support the child. When the talents are different, it is a greater challenge for the parent, but it is also a greater opportunity for the parent to grow. Suppose the father is a physician and the son is interested in mechanics. Rather than ignore the son's activities as something he knows nothing about, the father can let the son introduce him to a whole new world of information.

Adoptive children serve as a dramatic reminder that children do not belong to their parents. Children, whether biological or adoptive, belong to themselves. The role of parents is one of stewardship. We parents guide and direct other unique human beings. We do not mold clay in our own image nor direct puppets on strings. This is true of all children, but the adopted child can remind us of this perspective in a special way.

Who can help you with your feelings on adoption? First

176

of all, since you and your husband are contemplating becoming parents, you need to share your feelings openly with each other. One of you may have stronger reservations than the other, or you may have different problems. Friends who have adopted children will probably be eager to talk about adoption.

Adoption agencies generally offer an introductory program about adoption which you and your husband can attend along with other couples. Thus you can get more information without actually applying for adoption. Finally, an interview with a good child-welfare worker can be very helpful.

If you are interested only in a healthy white infant, an agency may simply put you on a long waiting list. If, on the other hand, you are interested in a hard-to-place child, an adoption worker is apt to inform you that your prospects for getting a child are better. By "hard-to-place" we mean *older* children, children of *mixed race, physically or emotionally handicapped* children or *sibling groups*. The worker can help you to explore your feelings about adoption, to determine what child would be right for you, to put you in touch with support groups of adoptive parents, and to follow up after the adoption.

The idea of support groups and follow-up is particularly helpful if you decide to adopt a hard-to-place child. You discover that other people have successfully and happily done what you are contemplating. You become interested in the needs of all children in a personal way, and you make wonderful friends to share both the problems and the joys that are ahead of you as adoptive parents.

# New Directions

Today the adoption picture is changing. Twenty years ago adoption was a way for childless couples to have a family.

Agencies tried to match a child as closely as possible with the adoptive parents. The looks, ethnic origins and even talents of the biological parents were examined carefully. When talented musicians applied for adoption, agencies would search for a child with a likelihood of musical talent.

Frequently children were not told they were adopted. Sometimes the revelation of this "secret" produced shock in the child who did not learn the truth until reaching adulthood. Adoption was considered second-best, to be hidden.

Today childless couples still seek adoption. However, there are very few infants available. The plain, if unpleasant, fact is that many babies are now aborted, and of the mothers who do give birth out of wedlock, 87 percent choose to keep the baby.

In this age of population concern, a new adage goes, "Never bring an unwanted child into the world." Paradoxically, the infant available for adoption is probably the most wanted child in the world today.

Despite the shortage of infants, many children are available for immediate adoption. Some may be older, frequently well into school age. They may be biracial or from another country. They may be mentally or physically handicapped. They may have been raised with brothers or sisters from whom it would be cruel to separate them.

All these children are waiting for a "forever" family. Most states maintain lists of waiting children.

All kinds of people adopt today including childless couples and families with their own biological children. Sometimes couples who have adopted one or two infants recognize that the "waiting" child offers them an opportunity to increase their family. Single persons also adopt. Often children do not resemble their adoptive parents. Further, the fact of adoption is not hidden but treated as a rather interesting, distinctive part of the child's heritage.

These parents adopt for the same reasons others have

children: They wish to be parents, to raise this particular child. Adoptive parents are not do-gooders, out to save unfortunate children. These parents frequently are baffled at the sympathetic approval they receive from outsiders who assume, wrongly, that self-sacrifice and pity are their motives.

A couple may decide to adopt a waiting child after meeting others who did so. Most states have an organization of adoptive parents to provide information, help and support to families who adopt waiting children. Familiarity with others makes the venture seem more possible.

Some waiting children are mentally or physically handicapped. People view handicaps in different ways. A family that values high academic achievement above all else might consider even mild retardation a severe burden and would never be comfortable adopting a retarded child.

Another family which has dealt with retardation, perhaps in a relative or close friend, might be excited by the potential of such a child. Similarly, deafness or a heart condition may not seem so severe to a particular family.

Research shows that the single, best predictor of how well a handicapped child will cope is the attitude of the parents toward the handicap rather than the handicap's severity. Parents who adopt a handicapped child must dwell on the child's potential.

Despite the variety of parents and children on the adoption scene today, we think most such families share a common bond. They all view adoption as an adventure. The adoptive parent feels lucky, perhaps a little smug. In a world where adoptive children are supposed to be in pitifully short supply, the adoptive parent thinks: "I looked a little harder, and I found a prize."

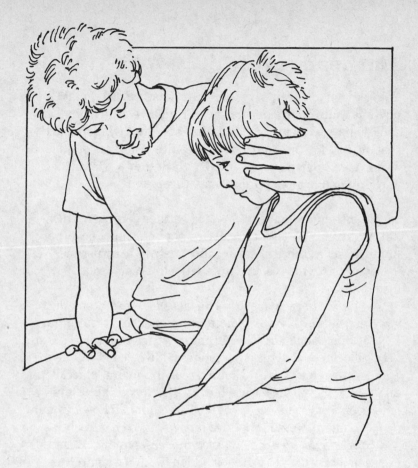

# Discipline

Discipline is all the ways parents mold the behavior of their children: rewarding some behaviors, ignoring some, and punishing still others. Parents need to keep in mind their goals for their children and to steer a fine path between authoritarianism and permissiveness. Parents need to change their approach as their children grow from babies who need to be held to teens who may need a behavior contract. The goal of discipline is to move the child from parent-control to self-control.

# The Kenny Credo

Your advice to parents on teen dating (see p. 101) makes it obvious that you are part of the permissive crowd of sociologists, educators, psychologists, etc., who are partly responsible for the increase in juvenile problems of all sorts. Your advice sounds like Hugh Hefner advising parents. I hope most parents saw through it.

As parents and columnists, we are neither permissive nor authoritarian. We reject the notion that one must be either harsh, strict authoritarian or kind, wishy-washy permissive. We want to try to give, in a nutshell, our credo about discipline:

1) *We mean what we say.* This goes for our statements to two-year-olds or 17-year-olds. A command from a parent to a child is like a contract. The parent must see that the request is carried out or lose his effectiveness. If we do not intend to enforce our request, we do not make it in the first place. After 20 years of parenting we are far from perfect. Like others we get lax or tired or hassled, but when we fail to follow through on a command, we know we are falling down on our job.

2) *We do not give orders we cannot enforce.* We do not tell our teenagers that they are forbidden to smoke cigarettes, smoke pot, drink or race in cars. We cannot control this behavior by authoritarian commands when the children are out of our presence. Forbidding leads to sneaking and denial on the part of children and to suspicion on the part of parents. If the behavior does occur, there is no way it can be discussed.

We do *not* condone such behaviors. We attempt to control them in ways that are more effective than giving orders. The first is good modeling: We don't smoke ourselves, we drink in moderation, and we are cautious in cars. We emphasize that our disapproval of drunkenness and racing stems from common sense and is not merely a parental hangup.

Furthermore, since these activities are not forbidden,

there is no game of sneaking or hiding. When they occur—
and at times they have in our family—we can talk about
them openly.

3) *We encourage behavior that is incompatible with the
unwanted behavior.* We value good health. Therefore, parents
and children jog, swim or exercise regularly. We do not
demand athletic achievement, but we applaud it when it
occurs.

4) *We do make rules that we can observe and enforce.*
These rules, include things such as, "Do the dishes." "Attend
school," and, "Be home by 11 o'clock."

Sometimes authoritarianism works. A parent might say,
"You will *never* smoke (or drink, smoke pot, etc.)," and the
child is so awed by the consequences that he or she never
does. Even when this strategy works, we reject it. When
children's compliance is purchased at the price of their failing
to make their own decisions and to discipline themselves, this
is too great a price.

Our ultimate goal for our children is independence. From
the earliest years we try to give as much real responsibility
as the child can handle. For younger children this includes
getting to places on time and remembering lunches,
homework and permission slips without reminders. For older
children it includes doing household jobs or getting a
substitute, managing money and choosing one's life goals and
schooling beyond high school. We agree with the state that
an 18-year-old is an adult, and we do not establish curfews or
rules of behavior for them.

Do our methods work? Four of our children have reached
the age of 18. Two of them, upon finishing high school, went
to live and work on their own in other cities. All have now
returned to school.

We feel confident of their ability to deal with problems.
We look forward to a phone call or visit from them, not to
give them advice, but to hear their fresh, new impressions of
what life is like. We are convinced that only when you

prepare your children for independence and, whatever the risks, give them some room to make decisions, make mistakes and grow, only then can you reap the reward of real communication with your children.

# Better, Not More, Discipline

**Don't you think today's parents are failing to discipline their children? I believe there needs to be *more* discipline in the home.**

Be careful not to confuse discipline with authoritarianism. To our mind, discipline is *all* the things parents do to mold the behavior of their children. This is a lot broader than giving orders and punishing disobedience. Discipline is getting your child to do what he or she is supposed to do—and that means all the reminding and the rules, the praise and the punishment it takes to accomplish that goal.

In general, there are three ways to discipline:

1) *To reward good behavior.* This is the best way of encouraging and strengthening behavior.

2) *To ignore bad behavior.* This is the best way of weakening undesirable behavior.

3) *To punish bad behavior.* Punishing has a mixed effect. It may be good at eliminating a specific bad behavior right now, but it is not very effective in the long run. In other words, punishment just tells the child to stop; it does not say what else to do.

Some parents attempt to discipline too much. Yet, the quality of discipline is more important than the quantity. Parents need to be reassured that not everything needs to be disciplined. They do not have to "cover the waterfront," or change the child in every way. It is usually sufficient to pick an area or two. No intelligent general would move his army uniformly along the front line. Rather he would pick a few strategic places to attack. Certainly he would pick places where he would be likely to win.

Parents sometimes need to remember that they are not molding a child in every detail; rather they are hoping to teach self-control. Consequently it is more important to do the job well in one or two areas than to struggle to control every behavior. This seemingly simple suggestion can be immensely relieving to the mother who finds herself screaming and nagging at her child all day.

What area or areas should a parent pick to discipline? Some areas are unimportant because the child will probably outgrow the troublesome behavior if left alone. Other areas (like eating, sleeping and learning) are almost impossible to discipline directly. Many a frustrated parent has learned the hard way that you can lead a child to books, but you cannot make him learn. The same hard fact applies to eating and sleeping.

The wise parent, like the intelligent general, picks areas where he or she can be effective. There is no answer to the question of which areas are most important. Families differ. To some parents table manners are important. To others, a regular bedtime for children is absolutely necessary for parental sanity.

It is obviously important to keep wet little fingers out of electric wall sockets and errant little feet out of streets. Certain family chores like dusting, table-setting, dishwashing, and trash-emptying are legitimate. Coming when called, refraining from clobbering brother with a ball bat, walking instead of running through the house, and many more are fair game. Just do not succumb to the temptation of multiplying regulations. Pick a few, insist on these with all your parental wile and wherewithal, and learn to tolerate the rest.

Children need some controls. Parents must help them control their own impulses. The point is that this is best done by controlling a few things well. Usually, the parent who tries to control too much is ineffective. Or worse, this parent may be too effective. Then we have the "good" child who is good, not because he or she behaves well, but because he or she does not behave at all. This parent has suppressed the misbehavior by unfortunately suppressing most of the child's activity.

In summary, we are not sure we need *more* discipline in the home, but we can always use *better* discipline.

# Beyond Punishment

Many people dislike the word *discipline*. The word conjures up images of rules, regimentation and especially punishment. Discipline seems to mean quelling a child's spirit.

Actually all parents discipline. When done well, discipline is a positive action. Discipline means all the things parents do or can do to mold the behavior of their children—all the reminding and the rules, the praise and the punishment, even the ignoring at appropriate times.

No one "right" way to discipline exists. There are many ways to reach a child. Some work better with one child; other ways work with another child, even in the same family. One way might work at a certain age. When the same child is older, other means are more effective. Following are some of the many ways parents can discipline:

1) *Prevent when possible:* This is the best discipline of all. Mother senses that hungry children are crabby children, ready to fight at the least provocation. Since dinner is still a half-hour away, she puts out cheese cubes and carrot sticks to nibble.

When her toddler grandson is coming to visit, Grandma puts all the figurines and ash trays out of reach. Prevention anticipates problems before they arise.

2) *Focus on the positive:* Setting a youngster up for success instead of failure is good discipline. Larry is a poor math

student. Rather than punish him because of his poor grades, Larry's dad points out the progress Larry is making in math. He looks for right answers on Larry's math papers and emphasizes the number of multiplication facts Larry has mastered. Dad also realizes that Larry will never be an engineer or accountant and avoids setting impossible goals for his son.

3) *Let the child suffer the consequences of behavior:* Allowing a child to experience the natural consequences of behavior is good discipline. Mother and Dad do not tell Linda she must not speed when she drives. Since they are not with her, they cannot control whether or not she speeds. They do, however, insist that she pay her own speeding tickets. Two $60 fines have slowed Linda up considerably.

4) *Set a good example:* Setting a good example can encourage good behavior and discourage the bad. Smoking, drinking, eating habits, exercise and attitudes toward religion are some areas where example counts.

Consequently, don't expect your child to be a non-smoker if you smoke.

Don't expect your child not to overindulge in alcohol or drugs if you overindulge in liquor from time to time.

Don't expect your child to eat a balanced diet if you have a habit of indulging in rich foods or if you go to the other extreme and constantly skip meals.

Don't expect your child to value exercise if your only exercise is getting up and down from the table and getting up from the sofa to switch the TV dial.

Don't expect your child to be religious if you do not attend Mass when you are supposed to, or if you ignore living your Christianity daily regardless of whether or not it seems sensible or convenient.

Good discipline is far more than suppressing and punishing children's action. Far from quelling their spirit, it makes them more controlled, considerate, loving and lovable human beings.

# 'Physical' Discipline

Recently the Supreme Court ruled that there is nothing unconstitutional about using physical punishment on children in school. The ruling brought criticism in the media. *Time* magazine published readers' letters deploring the decision. The Chicago *Tribune* wrote in an editorial: "It makes no ethical, legal, or common sense to tolerate corporal punishment against children when it is not permitted against any other group of people in our society....No recognized child-care expert advocates physical punishment. It is not a technique of discipline taught in schools of education. Not only is it mean and humiliating, it is also ineffective as a way of changing behavior."

We are against the abuse of children. We are not necessarily against spanking. The above editorial is typical of a very simplistic view of physical punishment. It fails to consider that verbal and mental abuses by parents and teachers can be more devastating than physical abuse. It is also incorrect because sometimes physical punishment is not abusive but appropriate.

We, of course, object to the mother in the store who pounds on her three-year-old out of frustration. We are firmly opposed to the father who, in righteous anger, beats up his 14-year-son who has just been caught smoking. Yet we have seen verbal attacks by parents and teachers that were far more destructive. Subtle criticism. Ridicule. Put-downs. Insulting and mean comments. A clever adult can destroy the self-image, the very soul of a child without ever touching him or her.

Every adult has school memories. Think back to your own childhood. Which ones stayed with you the longest, hurt the most? For most the real pain came from being shamed or embarrassed or from being ridiculed for failure. Those are the memories that still haunt us. Not the times we got our knuckles rapped or got hit on the shoulder with a pointer.

There is a difference between physical punishment and violence. We are not for violence. We are for physical punishment under certain conditions. Here's why.

Sometimes a spanking can be the most effective punishment. We know from psychology that adult time and attention are major rewards. Long lectures and nagging can actually be perceived by the child as a reward. They tend to encourage the very behavior they are supposed to eliminate. A spanking has minimal reward value for the child.

A spanking can also clear the air. The bad behavior has been attended to briefly and immediately. Now the matter is over. A good example might be a two-year-old who starts to toddle across the street. A verbal *no* plus a quick spank on the leg is a great improvement over a lecture and long explanation.

Actually spanking should be considered under the larger category of physical discipline. Other examples of physical discipline include restraining a rambunctious child, physically "helping" the procrastinator, going and getting a child reluctant to come, and letting certain behaviors suffer their natural consequences. The advantage to physical discipline is that the child receives little time and attention (secondary gain).

Finally, spanking can be a legitimate response to what Kohlberg describes as "stage one morality," that is, the level of pure self-interest where the child seeks pleasure and avoids pain. A spanking need not be a beating. It can be a simple touch-communication at the stage one level, and a painful one. Many children begin some growth beyond stage one by age four, although some 10-year-olds still behave like fours.

We think physical punishment is a seldom but sometime thing. Because of an adult penchant for losing one's temper, we'd like to suggest three simple safeguards:

1) *Never spank in anger.*

2) *Never spank without a witness.* This is as good a rule

for parents as it is for teachers. Ideally a sibling or spouse should be nearby.

3) *Don't spank after age four,* unless the child is behaving (misbehaving) at a preschool level. By this I mean impulsive, uninhibited, unplanned behavior. This would almost never be the case with a teen.

We are very much against child abuse, but we have seen the spoken word do more permanent damage than the moving hand. Paddling and knuckle-rapping are mild indeed compared to some verbal assaults we've had to witness.

# Discipline vs. Punishment

**Do you agree that children under four need more "pats" of discipline and over four more "psychology"?**

While it may seem we "pat" little ones and "psych out" older children, that impression needs some clarification. Using psychology does not mean we "out-psych" or "outwit" our children. Using psychology means we handle a child in the way best suited to his developmental level. We *always* try to use psychology.

It is true that we use physical discipline with the young child. We use it because it is the best way to get a message across to him. Physical discipline, however, does not necessarily mean punishment. Discipline is more than punishment. Discipline is all the ways we shape and control the behavior of our children. With the child from two to four, we use physical discipline frequently and punishment almost never. Here are some examples which illustrate the difference.

When you call your toddler, her normal reaction is to grin mischievously and run the other way. You simply go after her and physically bring her back. No spanking or punishment. You have used physical discipline to convey the message that parents mean what they say, a message which must be demonstrated to the child many times. It is crucially important throughout childhood.

When we take our three-year-old to the supermarket, he rides in the grocery cart even though he would prefer to roam free. We don't punish him but, because of our great respect for pyramids of pickle jars, we insist he rides. This is physical discipline.

When would we punish the young child? Never before he can really understand what *no* means. Before this time punishment is useless. Since it would bewilder him, it would probably be harmful as well.

We would use punishment under two conditions: First, when some very hazardous action is involved. If a two-year-old runs in the street, we would chase her, grab her and generally convey that we were very concerned. We might spank the leg that stepped into the street. The message we would try to convey is that this is not a run-and-chase game but a very serious danger. We would not, however, expect a two-year-old to grasp the danger even after this lesson. Developmentally she is not yet capable of grasping this fully. It would still be our responsibility to see she didn't go in the street.

The second occasion when we might use punishment is when the two- or three-year-old is deliberately testing us. For example:

Mom says, "Matt, don't touch that bowl. Those beaters can hurt you." With a sly little grin, Matt sticks his finger in near the moving beaters.

On this occasion, Mom would remove the hand and probably give one firm spank. The message is, "Mommy means business." We punish when we need adherence right now because of a clear danger to the child or to others.

We would never punish the young child for curiosity or accident. Pulling toys apart, spilling milk and breaking things are behaviors which exasperate parents. They are part

191

of life with a young child. We parents must be careful not to punish merely because we are irritated. Buy sturdier toys and use stronger plastic.

The occasions when behavior is clearly dangerous or defiant should be rather rare in young children. By using *punishment* sparingly, it can be effective on these occasions. The rest of the time use *physical discipline*. Remember that your child wants to please you. Take time to enjoy the happy, curious, interesting child that it is your privilege to raise.

# Rewards vs. Bribes

**You have written several times about being positive with children, about emphasizing the positive. You suggest that parents reward as well as punish. Isn't that like a bribe to be good? What other rewards can you suggest besides money and sweets?**

If being bad necessitates punishment, then being good deserves equal time. You can call it a bribe if you wish. But when people, big or little, do something worthwhile and nice, then some sort of recognition or applause is called for.

There are many ways to reward behavior besides money and sweets. Time and attention are the simplest, most important ways. When Dad sits with his son in the basement watching his son hammer a makeshift boat, he is giving his time to reward woodworking. When mother inquires about the details of a school success, she is paying attention.

Touch is another effective reinforcer. The coach who hugs a player after a good effort is rewarding the effort. The teacher who touches the shoulders of an active first grader in his seat may be encouraging sitting-in-your-seat behavior.

Praise is a mixed bag. It rewards, but it carries a subtle pressure to keep up the performance. It is not as effective as time, attention and touch.

You mention sweets. Candy, pop, cake and cookies are sometimes used as rewards. The sugar content of these foods, however, might well make you unhappy. Some alternatives might be nuts, popcorn or fruits.

The chance to learn can also be a reward for desirable behavior. Learning to play a musical instrument can be a reward. The child may welcome drawing lessons, the chance to work with tools, building models or working with clay. Learning to drive is important to the older teens.

Toys are an obvious reward. One parent had a grab bag of small toys which the child could select when things went well. Valued by most children are cars, dolls, games, bicycles and no end of other items.

Excursions can be eagerly worked for. They might include a ride in the car, going to work with Dad, going shopping with Mom, or visiting grandparents. How about a visit to the seashore, a train ride, an airplane ride, going out to dinner with your parents, visiting a friend, visiting a new city, visiting a museum, or even taking a walk in the woods and hunting for frogs or birds or leaves or leprechauns?

Entertainment is always popular. Going to a movie, watching a favorite TV program, listening to a special record, or putting on a play or puppet show for parents can be a reward for good behavior.

Sports and games are attractive. Playing ball with Dad, swimming, bike riding, skating, horseback riding, Ping-Pong, and fishing can all be used. Table games like chess, checkers, and Monopoly are also popular. Believe it or not, helping around the house can be rewarding. Some children are eager to set the table, make beds, paint a room, do minor repairs and run errands. Baking cookies, picking flowers (even when unasked), and working in the garden may also be a treat. Older children usually see these as chores, but the younger ones are often eager to help.

Playing with friends, going to scouts, and having friends over may be a social bonus. Staying up past bedtime, having a pet, and having a party are also worth working for, not to mention use of the car, getting new clothes, putting on makeup, or going to a beauty parlor. The objects and activities used as rewards can be as varied as the ages and interests of our children.

Rewards are like "gold stars" given to let our children know we value what they are doing. Time and attention are at the core. They tell our children when they are doing well.

# How to Reward

Frequently we advocate rewarding your child. We suggest that supporting the good in a person is more pleasant and more effective than punishing the bad. Some people disagree. They caution against rewarding children for behavior. The difference lies in the understanding of rewards. Reward, for them, means handing out prizes as though life were some sort of giant television give-away show. We too would discourage such an approach. What we mean by reward, however, is saying to your child in word or action, "Good job. I approve of you. You are fine."

Certain qualities distinguish good rewards for children:

First, the reward occurs close to the good behavior. The child who picks up his room gets a gold star right away, not whenever mother gets to the store to buy them. The child who had been promised an overnight guest if he did his homework every night for a week has his guest on Friday night, not a week later. The older the child, the longer delay he can tolerate. But rewards that are delayed too long go stale.

Second, the reward is earned. If the child falls short in some way, no reward is given. If the child gets dessert only when the meal is finished, then there is no dessert when he or she *almost* finishes.

Third, rewards are in proportion to the behavior. If

mother comments five times because Johnny made his bed once, Johnny will wonder what all the fuss is about. In the future he is apt to be skeptical about mother's enthusiasm. One comment is probably enough.

Rewards should also be realistic. If a young athlete has never finished a race in the top three, do not promise a 10-speed bike for winning. Such emphasis on winning discourages rather than supports because it demands performance beyond the child's present capabilities. Much more supportive is the parent who says, "You ran your best time ever? Terrific!"

Finally, rewards are given generously. Frequently parents say, "Why should I compliment my son for taking out the trash. That's his job. Of course he is supposed to do it." Doing what you are supposed to is what makes responsible people, and responsibility makes for a smoother world. Being responsible is no small achievement. Notice it.

Most of the worthwhile things that you or we or our children do are precisely modest but necessary tasks faithfully performed—tasks like taking out the trash. They can so easily go unnoticed, yet each of us gets a lift when someone notices and cares that we have done our job. When your child does what he is supposed to, do not get out the account book. Do not ponder whether a reward is deserved. Notice the behavior. Give a compliment. Appreciate him or her, and give a pat on the back. We all need one from time to time.

# What to Ignore

When parents think of controlling children, they usually think first of *punishment.* In desperation they may next turn to *rewards.* But parents still have a third option, one which is highly effective and frequently misunderstood. If you want certain behavior to stop, *ignore it.* A child would rather have his behavior criticized than ignored. Behavior that does not get attention tends to die out.

What kind of behavior can you ignore? That depends on the age of the child and your choices as a parent. Here are some general principles as guides:

1) *Never ignore babies.* A baby is trying to get your attention because something is wrong. This is vital communication. Answer.

2) *Ignore crude body behavior in young children.* Little ones delight in learning to burp, grunt or make weird sounds. Like handling parts of the body, it represents their effort to discover more about their own bodies. It disappears quickest if ignored. (If you do not believe that ignoring works, notice how quickly such behavior increases when older brothers and sisters laugh and roar their approval.)

3) *Ignore language shockers in preschool and primary-level children* after saying, "I don't want you to say that any more."

4) *Ignore bickering among elementary school children when possible.* A report that "Timmy is pulling Sally's hair out by the roots" cannot be easily ignored. Decide quickly: Is the report accurate? Is real harm being done? Can I improve the situation by intervening? If your answers are no, ignore the complaint.

5) *Ignore arguments from preteens and teens.* Children at this age can overwhelm parents by demanding permissions and privileges and rule changes: "Why can't I stay overnight with Susie?" "Why can't I have a new pair of jeans?" "Why can't I use the car?"

The questioners do not want an explanation. They want their own way. Weigh the request and decide on an answer. Then, if you have decided the answer is no, say so and give your reason. If argument follows, as it often will, then ignore it.

6) *Pay attention to your child's thoughts, questions, accomplishments, interests, good behavior.*

# Behavior Contracts

You describe using "behavior contracts" to solve problems between parent and child. This sounds very unloving to me. I think the love of a husband and wife and the love of parent and child should be beyond something so mechanical as a contract. This bothers me. Please comment.

You are absolutely right. Love does not need contracts. But if love were always the predominant emotion, we would not need marriage contracts either. Love turns obligation into a joy. We all know that children sometimes resent house rules. Wives sometimes get mad at forgetful or neglectful husbands. If these negative feelings result in an impasse, a "contract" can get you back in business.

Yes, contracts are unloving. That does not mean they are hateful. Rather, they are a mechanical, neutral strategy devoid of emotion. They are useful for unloving moments in a relationship, when love momentarily breaks down. Like any other contract, they impose obligations on both sides. For example, the plumber fixes the sink. The homeowner then pays the bill. That's a contract—necessary because the plumber and homeowner are not motivated by love for each other.

Let me give two very simple examples, one parent-child and one husband-wife. Take a case where the 15-year-old daughter is staying out past her "curfew" and has started to skip school. The parents get a letter from the principal advising them of their responsibility. The parents respond by "grounding" their daughter, keeping her home until further notice. Daughter is furious and threatens to leave home. Then she lapses into a week or two of bitter silence punctuated only by an occasional mean remark. The parents feel both anger and concern. They are angry that their daughter does not behave better and concerned that they may be losing her. Things are quite unpleasant.

This is where a behavior contract can be helpful. Each side must give up something. The parents are most concerned about the truancy, but they also want their daughter to be at home at a reasonable hour. The daughter says she can't stand being "grounded" and wants time to be with her friends. So they negotiate.

A family faced with the above problem arrived at the following agreement. The daughter promised to attend school every day. Parents would verify this. In return, daughter could stay out until 10:00 p.m. each night. If she failed to attend school, she agreed to work two hours around the home instead of going out that night.

Further, if the daughter got home on time at night, she was given a bonus point. Each bonus point was worth an extra half hour out. In other words, in return for daughter coming home when she was supposed to, parents agreed to give her extra time out according to the contract. If she was late, she had to do a half-hour's work for every 15 minutes late.

Different families would negotiate different details, but the above contract got one family out of an emotional logjam. It worked. They are friends again. Daughter is not truant, and she is home more than she was before.

A common and basic husband-wife problem is that one likes to go to bed early and the other is a late-nighter. This situation can go from being humorous to occasioning considerable antagonism. One couple we know reached the point where they began to see very little of each other. He went to bed early in the evening. She stayed up until midnight. Heaven help her if she woke him then.

Finally they negotiated a compromise. She agreed to go to bed early with him two nights a week. He stayed up late with her two nights. The other three nights they did what they felt like at the time. Among other things, their sex life improved considerably. Apparently love was not enough to get her to bed early or keep him up late each night. It took the device of a verbal contract to help love along.

In love one gives 100 percent. By contrast, a behavior contract arranges a 50-50 settlement. Sometimes it takes just such a strategy to break the mean and negative stalemate. Love then has a chance to renew itself.

# When Parents Disagree

What do you do when husband and wife disagree about the discipline of the children? We have four teenage daughters. My husband doesn't believe in consistency of discipline nor having children earn privileges or money. Every question is answered O.K., and they are just handed money for the asking. He doesn't even question what it is for. I believe that inconsistency of discipline and disagreements (frequent and loud) over children and their lack of responsibilities is a bad home situation. It's the only arguing we do.

You have brought up a difficult situation. When husband and wife differ in style (he's easy-going; she's rather strict), but still agree on basic principles of childraising, they are apt to be successful. What you describe, however, is a basic difference in handling children. It is doubly difficult for you because it is hard to be the "heavy," the one who does all the "no" saying.

The suggestion we are about to make will sound strange unless you believe as we do that change can only be built on positive factors. Arguing simply does not work. No amount of discussion is going to show your husband the "error of his ways." So what do you do?

Our suggestion is to relax and join him. Do not insist on jobs, hours, good grades, or any such responsibilities. Are we advising you to cop out, to neglect all your responsibilities as a parent? We don't think so. We simply do not think you can be effective working against your husband. Trying to do so only puts you on edge and frustrates you terribly, none of which, as you say, adds to a happy home life. Extreme permissiveness is not good for children but, in your situation, it is better than working at cross purposes with your husband.

At the same time, notice all the good things about your husband. Try writing them down. Apparently he is quite generous, loving and easy-going. Notice these things and make sure he and your daughters know you are aware of his virtues and really appreciate them. A generous, loving, easy-going man around the house is no small blessing.

What we are saying is that, while teaching responsibility to children is important, developing a loving household is even more important. When you and your husband are in harmony, you may find opportunities to introduce greater consistency in discipline. Suppose, for example, your husband eventually does express some concern about the girls' late hours, poor grades, or extravagance with money. You might respond that you too are concerned, but you realize that nothing much can be done until you both agree on some sort of program to deal with the behavior. If you can develop an atmosphere where you and your husband are working together to solve a problem instead of arguing about the solution, you are on the way to constructive discipline.

If Dad never does display concern over the girls' behavior, you might try to pick an area—and only one—which you think most needs correcting. Then tell him straight out how you feel about the hours the girls keep on weekend nights: "I think they are too young to set their own hours. I need you to help me figure out what hours they should keep and to enforce them. I can't do it alone."

With such a direct message you might get his support or, at the very least, he might respond with his feelings on the subject. By sharing your feelings you might find some common ground for working together.

The problem you describe has no easy solution. Your husband's behavior is not within your control. Therefore work on developing what is largely under your control—a happy, loving household.

# Unconditional Love

**It is nice to be positive with children, but too much praise will make children conceited, and that's not a desirable Christian value. Besides life will cut them down plenty soon. It's better not to build them up. Otherwise it's too much of a comedown later.**

Harvey Cox has described Church as a place where Christians gather to "lick their wounds." We think home should be like that too. Home is the one place you can go and count on being accepted for what you are.

Erich Fromm divided love into "conditional" love and "unconditional" love. Conditional, or father-love, says: If you do things right, I love you. Stay dry at night. Be nice to sister. Get good grades in school. Catch the ball. Do these things and you will be loved.

Unconditional, or mother-love, says: I love you for what you are. Simply because you are 10. Blonde. A girl. Annie. I love you, no questions asked. Love, just for being you.

Both parents give both kinds of love. Father-love and mother-love should both be found in a home. But mother-love may well be found nowhere else.

The very fact that life cuts everyone down simply reinforces the need to find unconditional love in the home. Children and other humans act out how they feel. A positive self-image forms the very basis of mental health. You must love yourself to be able to love others. This basic self-love is what provides you with the confidence to give yourself to others in service.

The basic self-love we are talking about does not mean spoiling or a false pride. In fact, this constructive self-love forms the groundwork for self-discipline, for humility, for generosity, for altruism. You must feel good about yourself before you can reach out easily to others.

Where do children get a good self-image? They read it in the eyes of significant others—especially parents, but teachers and friends too. They find it in a look that accepts, a touch that says you're beautiful, a word that enlivens.

Alfred Adler felt the basic cause of mental illness was a feeling of inferiority—a feeling that we don't know why we're here; where we're going; we have little control over our own life; we are flawed. We can overcompensate for our inferiority feelings by high achievement. But the only factor that truly makes it tolerable is unconditional love.

We think we should discipline our children. We are not permissive. At the same time we don't think it is possible to be too nice, to praise children too much, to love them more than is good for them. Mother-love leads to a good, solid self-image. Persons with a good self-image think well of themselves and behave well. They are more ready to love others.

Now that we reflect on it, God the Father behaves rather wisely. The only catch is that, in his loving, he (she?) behaves more like a mother.

# Index